Effective Adoption Panels

Guidance on regulations, process and good practice in adoption and permanence panels in England

Jenifer Lord
Deborah Cullen
Revised by Elaine Dibben

Published by
CoramBAAF Adoption and Fostering Academy
41 Brunswick Square
London WC1N 1AZ
www.corambaaf.org.uk

Coram Academy Limited registered as a company limited by guarantee in England and Wales number 9697712, part of the Coram group, charity number 312278

Originally published by BAAF 1997
Second edition 2000
Third edition 2006
Fourth edition 2009
Fifth edition 2012
Sixth edition 2013
Seventh edition published by CoramBAAF in 2016
© CoramBAAF 2016

British Library Cataloguing in Publication Data
A catalogue record for this book is available from the British Library

ISBN 978 1 910039 51 9

Project management by Shaila Shah, Director of Publications, CoramBAAF
Designed and typeset by Helen Joubert Design
Printed in Great Britain by The Lavenham Press

All rights reserved. Except as permitted under the Copyright, Designs and Patents Act 1988, this publication may not be reproduced, stored in a retrieval system, or transmitted in any form or by any means, without the prior written permission of the publishers.

The moral right of the authors has been asserted in accordance with the Copyright, Designs and Patents Act 1988.

Contents

Introduction	**1**
Current regulations and guidance	1
How this guide will help you	2
How this guide is structured	2
Using this guide	2
Appendices	3
1 Establishing the panel	**4**
Requirement to have an adoption panel	4
The central list and panel – the regulations	4
Membership of a joint adoption panel	4
Frequency of panel meetings	4
Membership – practice issues	4
The central list	5
Appointment to sit on a panel	5
Chair	5
Social work members	6
Elected members (local authority) or director, manager or other officer of a voluntary adoption agency	7
Medical adviser	7
Independent panel members	7
Vice-chair	7
Agency adviser to the panel	7
Legal advice	8
Attendance of non-panel members at panel meetings	8
Quorum	9
Appointment of substitutes	9
Recruitment to the central list	9
Central list and panel membership agreement	10
Checks on central list and panel members	10
Induction and training	11
Review of central list and panel members	11
Adoption panel fees	12
Tenure of office of members of the central list and adoption panel	12
Resignation by central list and panel members	12
Termination of appointment of central list and panel members	13
Adoption panel functions	13
Adoption and permanence panel and concurrent planning and Fostering for Adoption (FFA)	14
Adoption reports	15
Declaring an interest	15
Reaching a recommendation	15
The decision-maker	16
Agency decision-making	16
Administration	17
Disclosure of minutes	18
Electronic communication	19
Monitoring and review	19
Adoption inspection	19
2 Agency policy and practice issues	**20**
Making the adoption process work well	20
Duties in relation to adoption	20
The "welfare checklist" in relation to adoption	20
Achieving good policies and practice in adoption work	21
Adoption panel policies and procedures	22
The panel's involvement in contributing to good practice	22
Specific issues that panel members will need to consider	22
Family structures	23
References	23
Criminal background	24
Health and disability issues	24
Lesbian and gay issues	25
Discipline issues	25

Matching policy in relation to culture, "race", religion and language	26
Permanence	26
Contact	27
Health and safety issues	27
Financial matters	27
Family work patterns	27
Adoption support services	27
Placements with family members or existing foster carers	27
Members of staff	28
Duration of approval	28
Representations and complaints	28

3 Considering adoption for a child — 30

Introduction	30
Adoption plans for children – the involvement of a court	30
The panel's role in adoption plans for children	31
Relinquishment for adoption of an infant aged less than six weeks	31
Panel functions	31
Timescales	31
Information required	32
Legal advice	32
People attending the panel	32
Welfare of children	32
The child's permanence report	33
Issues to consider	33
Permanence options	37
Practice considerations in relation to permanence options	38
Contact issues	38
Giving advice on whether a placement order should be applied for	39
Conditional or "in principle" recommendations	40

What next?	40
Flowchart: Routes by which a child comes to panel with a proposed adoption plan	41

4 Families offering placements — 42

Introduction	42
Function of the panel	42
The range of families to be considered	42
Preparation and assessment process and timescales	43
Information required for a full report	44
Checks and references required	46
The prospective adopter's report	46
Reports to the adoption panel	47
Legal advice	47
Conditional or "in principle" recommendations	47
Brief report	47
Applicants attending the panel	48
Issues to consider	48
Preparation, training and support	49
Strengths needed	49
Issues relating to the family	49
Issues relating to meeting the child's needs	51
Range of approval	53
Decision-making process	53
Review and termination of approval	53
Flowchart: Families offering placements – from first enquiry to approval	54
What next?	55

5 Matching children with families — 56

Panel functions	56
Process by which the proposed match has reached the panel	56
Timescales	57
Authorisation to place for adoption	57

Child already living with the family	57
Information required	58
Legal advice	59
Attendance at the panel	59
Welfare of children	59
Issues to consider	59
Adoption support services	61
Contact arrangements	62
Parental responsibility	63
Baby placements where the child is relinquished for adoption	63
Flowchart: Process for identifying a family after a decision that a child should be placed for adoption	**64**
Reaching a recommendation on a proposed match	65
What next?	65

6 Intercountry adoption — 67

Introduction	67
Agency policies and procedures	67
Considering and deciding whether a child should be placed for adoption outside the British Islands	67
Considering whether a child should be placed for adoption in a Hague Convention country	68
The panel's involvement in considering a match with approved adopters from a Hague Convention country	69
The panel's involvement in children's cases when the Hague Convention is not in force in the overseas country	69
Considering prospective adopters	70
Issues relating to the family	70
Change of approval	72
Post-placement and post-adoption support	72

Appendix I: Context of the agency's placement work — 73

Local authorities	73
Voluntary agencies	74

Appendix II: Acts of Parliament, Statutory Instruments and Government Guidance — 75

Introduction to Adoption: National Minimum Standards 2014 — 77

Appendix III: Glossary of terms — 78

Appendix IV: Useful organisations — 84

Appendix V: Sample job descriptions, evaluation and review formats — 86

Sample job description and person specification for central list and panel members	86
Sample central list and adoption panel membership agreement	87
Review of central list and panel members	89
Sample self-evaluation form: central list and panel member	90
Sample review form: central list and panel members	92
Sample job description and person specification for panel Chair	93
Sample adoption panel Chair agreement	95
Review of panel Chair	97
Sample self-evaluation form: panel Chair	98
Sample review form: panel Chair	100
Checklist of additional information that may be provided by the agency	101

Book list — 102

Acknowledgements

The original edition of *Effective Panels*, published in 1997, drew on the experience and expertise of members of a working party. Others with personal or professional experience of adoption were also consulted and all were acknowledged in the original and subsequent editions.

Subsequent editions as well as this one have drawn on the experience of CoramBAAF's consultants who chair or are members of panels, as well as those who attend CoramBAAF's Panel Chairs Group.

Elaine Dibben and Alexandra Conroy Harris, both of CoramBAAF, updated the 2013 edition. This edition has been revised by Elaine Dibben.

Notes about the authors

Jenifer Lord was a Child Placement Consultant for BAAF Southern England. She has chaired an adoption panel, and is currently a member of another one. She is also the author of *Adopting a Child* and *The Adoption Process*, and co-author of *Effective Fostering Panels*.

Deborah Cullen was the Legal Group Co-ordinator at BAAF for nearly 30 years. An expert in her field, she was a regular contributor to the journal *Adoption & Fostering*, as well as other journals, and authored several articles and books on child care law. She was the co-author of the first edition of this guide, then titled *Effective Panels*, published in 1997 and was involved in subsequent editions until she retired. Sadly, Deborah Cullen passed away in 2013.

Elaine Dibben started her social work career in residential social work and qualified in 1988. She has over 25 years experience of working in adoption and fostering in local authority and voluntary adoption agency settings. She joined BAAF in 2004 to become manager of the Independent Review Mechanism, which she set up and ran until 2009, when she moved to take on a wider role in BAAF as a trainer/consultant. She is currently an Adoption Development Consultant for CoramBAAF, alongside acting as a panel Chair for both adoption and fostering panels. She has authored several guides including *Undertaking an Adoption Assessment* (2013) and *Adoption by Foster Carers* (2016, with Viv Howorth).

Introduction

All adoption agencies, both local authority and voluntary, have been required to have adoption panels since the Adoption Agencies Regulations 1983 came into force in 1984. From December 30 2005, when the Adoption and Children Act 2002 was implemented in full, new regulations replaced these.

Current regulations and guidance

The principal regulations governing adoption work in England are the **Adoption Agencies Regulations 2005**. However, the **Adoption Agencies and Independent Review of Determinations (Amendment) Regulations 2011** replace Regulations 3 to 10 of the Adoption Agencies Regulations 2005, as amended, from 1 April 2011. These eight regulations are the ones covering panels. The **Adoption Agencies (Panel and Consequential Amendments) Regulations 2012** further amend the 2005 regulations, with effect from 1 September 2012, by prohibiting a panel's involvement in considering a child's adoption plan in cases where a court would be considering the making of a placement order. The **Adoption Agencies (Miscellaneous Amendments) Regulations 2013** set out a new framework for the assessment of prospective adopters with effect from 1 July 2013. The **Care Planning, Placement and Case Review and Fostering Services (Miscellaneous Amendments) Regulations 2013** regulate Fostering for Adoption, with a new temporary approval of prospective adopter as foster carer.

There is revised **statutory Adoption Guidance**, which was issued in July 2013, with a new Chapter 3 on work with prospective adopters. Further **draft Statutory Guidance** was issued in 2014 for consultation arising from the Children and Families Act 2014 (2014 Act) to reflect changes. However, at the time of this revision it has not been finalised and is likely to be further revised once the Children and Social Work Act is passed. **National Minimum Standards for Adoption** were issued in 2011 and some revisions were made in 2014 to reflect changes in the 2014 Act. These, and other relevant sets of regulations, are listed in Appendix II. Reference is made to the 2013 Statutory Guidance, by chapter number and section (for example, Chapter 3 section 29 is 3.29), but the Draft 2014 Statutory Guidance will be referenced where it is more relevant. Reference is made to the National Minimum Adoption Standards as NMS and the standard number. The regulations are referred to, in the main, by their initials (see list in Appendix II).

One change introduced in 2011 is that panels no longer have a fixed membership. Instead, agencies must establish a **central list** of people from which the membership of the panel, each time it meets, is chosen. In practice, many agencies have established a core group of panel members from the central list who attend most panel meetings, with other central list members attending from time to time. The same chairperson, who must be independent of the agency, will usually be appointed to each panel. There must be at least one social worker present and there will often be a medical adviser and usually a number of independent members who are likely to include an adoptive parent and an adopted adult. This diverse group of people, pooling and sharing their different experience and expertise, can speak from a very informed perspective and with an authoritative voice, providing a vital scrutiny as well as a validation of the agency's work.

Over the years, panels have changed and developed in the way they work. Prospective adopters must now be invited to attend panel whenever their case is being considered and many panels will also invite prospective adopters to the matching panel. Making sure that the views of birth parents and of the child are made clearly known to the panel is an essential consideration too.

Effective Adoption Panels acknowledges the vital role that panels play in relation to children needing adoption, their birth families, and their adoptive parents and foster carers. It aims to help panels to make sound and effective recommendations. Panels have an extremely important role to play within agencies and are expected to provide expert advice to adoption agencies, and to contribute to the development of policies and procedures.

Their key role is:

- to provide an independent scrutiny of the proposals presented and to determine
  - whether all the issues have been appropriately clarified; and
  - whether the proposal is sound.

How this guide will help you

This guide will be of interest and value not only to new and existing central list and panel members in England but also to all those who come into contact with the work of panels, particularly social workers, agency managers, committee members, adoptive parents and foster carers, and a wide range of other professionals.

For central list and panel members themselves, the key aims of this guide are:

- to inform them about their roles and responsibilities;
- to update them on current legislation and issues of good practice;
- to help them integrate this work within their own agency context and policies;
- to equip them with the knowledge, understanding and confidence needed to make appropriate recommendations in the best interests of children;
- to encourage them to play a full role as individual panel members and to continue to learn more about this task.

It is essential that central list and panel members are also given opportunities for regular training. It is hoped that the guide will alert agency staff and members to some of the issues that it would be helpful to cover more fully in training sessions.

How this guide is structured

We have organised this guide into six chapters followed by appendices.

Establishing the panel describes the range of cases that the panel may deal with, the central list and panel membership, and the role of each member. It outlines the terms and conditions of membership and the process for reaching a recommendation on individual cases. The panel's wider role and the importance of good administration and training are also discussed.

Agency policy and practice issues considers the panel's role in helping the agency draw up policies and procedures for adoption work within the context of the agency's wider work. It also describes specific issues that the panel will need to consider and on which clear policies or practice guidance may be useful. Current good practice and findings from research are described.

Considering adoption for a child whose parents consent and for whom a placement order is not required is one of the tasks of the panel. This chapter describes the range of factors that panel members will need to take into account before reaching their recommendation. It alerts them to the importance of checking on the progress of work with and on behalf of the child once the adoption plan has been agreed. There is a flow chart that sets out what will have happened before the case comes to the panel.

Families offering placements describes the issues that the panel will need to consider and take into account before making its recommendation as to whether an applicant is suitable to be an adoptive parent. It describes the Independent Review Mechanism (IRM). It also alerts panel members to the importance of reviewing the situation of waiting approved applicants. A flow chart sets out the stages in the process of work with families, both before and after the panel's recommendation.

Matching children and families describes the different ways in which matches may be made. It outlines the range of factors that panel members will need to consider before making a recommendation on whether a prospective adopter would be a suitable adoptive parent for a particular child. It also alerts panel members to the importance of receiving information on and of reviewing placements that have been made. A flow chart sets out what will have happened before the match comes to the panel.

Intercountry adoption Many, although not all, panels will consider the cases of families who are hoping to adopt from overseas. This chapter describes the process of intercountry adoption and the particular and different role of the panel in these cases. Panel members are alerted to the particular issues that they should consider, over and above those that they would consider in domestic adoption cases. Panels also have a role in considering whether a looked after child should be placed for adoption overseas and in considering a match, and issues involved in these considerations are described.

Using this guide

Effective Adoption Panels is designed both to be read from start to finish and also to be dipped into as particular issues arise. To enable readers to follow up issues more fully, each chapter includes cross-

Introduction

references to other chapters and ends with a list of references to research findings. Many of the books and articles mentioned are published by CoramBAAF and are easily available. CoramBAAF also produces a range of leaflets for the different parties attending panel and these are made available free to members and member agencies in the members' area of the CoramBAAF website (www.corambaaf.org.uk).

A list of all the Acts, Regulations and Guidance and Standards mentioned is provided in Appendix II. Each agency will have copies of these, and many of them can be downloaded from the Department for Education website at www.education.gov.uk.

Useful organisations are also listed in the appendices as is a glossary of terms. Throughout this guide, the term "children" refers to both children and young people. Similarly, we have used the term "applicants" to refer to prospective adopters who could be single, married, or in a partnership.

Appendices

The appendices of this book contain some supplementary information that agencies will find useful. This includes:

- Context of the agency's placement work
- Values statement that underpins the National Minimum Standards for Adoption
- Sample: Job description and person specification for central list and panel members
- Sample: Agreement form for central list and adoption panel members
- Sample: Review format for central list and panel members
- Sample: Job description and person specification for the Chair
- Sample: Agreement form for the Chair
- Sample: Review format for the Chair
- Checklist for additional information
- A list of useful books for further reading

Your agency may wish to use the job descriptions, person specifications, agreement forms and review formats that we have provided, or adapt them, or use their own material.

A pocket has been provided on the inside back cover, and we hope that you will use this to store other relevant information obtainable from the agency, as advised in this guide.

Establishing the panel

Requirement to have an adoption panel

Unless otherwise stated, the regulations referred to in this chapter are the Adoption Agencies and Independent Review of Determinations (Amendment) Regulations 2011.

Regulation 4 (1) requires that 'the adoption agency must constitute one or more adoption panels, as necessary'.

Regulation 4 (3) allows that 'any two or more local authorities may jointly constitute an adoption panel'.

There is no provision for voluntary adoption agencies (VAA) to establish joint panels. However, Guidance 1.35 states that different branches of the same VAA may share a panel.

The central list and panel – the regulations

Regulation 3 states that the agency 'must maintain a list of persons who are considered by it to be suitable to be members of an adoption panel (the "central list")'. Included on it must be:

- one or more social workers who have at least three years' relevant post-qualifying experience;
- the medical adviser to the adoption agency (or at least one if more than one medical adviser is appointed).

Regulation 4 requires that the agency must appoint from the central list:

- a person to chair the panel, who is independent of the agency;
- one or two people as Vice-chairs, who may act as Chair, if necessary.

Regulation 6 requires that no business may be conducted unless the following meet as a panel:

- the Chair or one of the Vice-chairs;
- a social worker, as defined in Regulation 3;
- three (or for a joint panel, four) other members. If the Chair is not present and the Vice-chair is not independent, then at least one other panel member must be an independent person.

Membership of a joint adoption panel

There is no difference between a joint panel and a single one except that the membership must be agreed by the agencies and the quorum must include four rather than three "other members", making a total of six members. Agencies will probably share a central list of potential panel members. Guidance on joint panels is given in 1.35.

Frequency of panel meetings

There is guidance on this in 1.26: 'Adoption panels must not be the "bottleneck" in the decision-making process. They must meet frequently and be able to meet at short notice before the next scheduled meeting to deal with urgent cases.' NMS 17.3 specifies that adoption panels should meet at least monthly unless it is an adoption panel of a small voluntary adoption agency, when it should meet six-weekly.

Membership – practice issues

Panels do not have a fixed membership or a maximum number of members. Guidance 1.28 states that: 'Each agency must maintain a list of persons whom it considers suitable to be members of an adoption panel. There is no limit to the number of people who may be included on the central list.' Guidance 1.42 requires that: 'When constituting an adoption panel the agency must draw members from the central list. These members must have the appropriate qualifications and/or experience to consider the cases submitted to the adoption panel.' The same people do not need to be appointed to every panel meeting. Subject to each meeting being quorate, Guidance 1.42 states: 'It is for the agency to decide how many panel members should be present at each panel meeting. However, a panel should not be so large as to make it difficult to chair the meeting or intimidating for those attending the meeting.'

Possibly a greater concern is that the panel may only ever be just quorate with not more than the required number of people being appointed to make it so. It would be particularly unfortunate if this resulted in the independent and service user experience and expertise being diminished. Guidance 1.19 states that panels 'are intended to be multi-disciplinary bodies with a considerable element of independence from the agency...Panels play an important quality assurance role, providing objectivity and having the ability to challenge practice which is felt not to be in the interests of children or falls short of the regulations or NMS.'

The central list

As described in more detail elsewhere in this chapter, all persons on the central list must have full checks, must be given induction and training, and must have a written panel agreement and an annual review of their performance. Although there is no limit to the number of people on the list, it is likely to work best, both from the agency's and the person's point of view, if it is small enough to give everyone the opportunity to be involved with the agency and to be invited on a regular basis to attend panel. There is no tenure requirement but, as discussed in the section on tenure, it will be important to ensure that new members are added to the list from time to time. In order for the list not to become unmanageably large, this will mean people coming off the list from time to time. There is no formal guidance on there being an ethnically diverse group of people on the central list or panel, but this would be good practice, as would having members who reflect the local community.

Appointment to sit on a panel

Guidance 1.28 states that: 'Having a pool of people with different skills, experience and qualifications allows for the most appropriate members to be drawn upon to consider individual cases and reduces the likelihood of panel meetings having to be postponed, whilst retaining knowledgeable and experienced members without the need for a vacancy to occur to appoint a new member to the list.'

There is no requirement to have a fixed membership on panel. However, as stated in the guidance for fostering panels, which are set up in the same way, 'the ability of the panel to function cohesively and with a level of consistency must be taken into account. This may be best achieved by having at least a core membership'. Experience suggests that the panel is likely to function best if most members know each other and are used to working as a group. Cases can recur with people approved to adopt subsequently coming back to panel to be matched with a child. It can be helpful if the same panel members are involved in these considerations.

Agencies should have written procedures on how and by whom decisions are made about who to appoint to a particular panel. It is important that this is seen to be transparent, fair and consistent.

Chair

The requirement to appoint an independent Chair from the central list to chair the panel is in Regulation 4. A person is not independent if they are:

- in the case of a registered adoption society, a trustee or employee of that society;

- in the case of a local authority:
    - an elected member of that authority; or
    - employed by that authority in the adoption service or for the purposes of any of that local authority's functions relating to the protection or placement of children;

- in either case, the adoptive parent of a child placed by that agency or an adoptive parent approved by that agency, even if the child is placed by another agency, unless at least 12 months have elapsed since an adoption order was made in respect of the child.

Regulation 4 specifies that the Chair must have the 'skills and experience' necessary to chair. Guidance 1.30 details the most significant qualities as being:

- 'a sound understanding of the adoption process;
- the authority and competence to chair a panel;
- the ability to analyse and explain complex information;
- the ability to identify key issues, problems and solutions;
- excellent interpersonal, oral and written communication skills.'

The Guidance continues that if the Chair does not possess 'a sound understanding of the adoption process but possesses all the other qualities, they may be appointed provided the agency considers that they will quickly develop an understanding of the adoption process and the agency ensures that the panel Chair receives appropriate training before taking up their appointment.'

- Guidance details key aspects of the Chair's role. He or she
    - should make it clear that every member's view is as valid as others, and should encourage everyone to participate and contribute to the panel's recommendations (Guidance 1.44);
    - is responsible for ensuring the accuracy of the panel's recommendations, reasons and, following agreement with panel members, the minutes (Guidance 1.45);
    - must make sure that a person who is not a member of the panel fulfils the task of writing these documents (Guidance 1.45).
- Where panel members have serious reservations, the Chair must ensure these are recorded in the minutes and are attached to the panel's recommendation (Guidance 1.46).
- If the panel cannot reach a consensus on its recommendation after the Chair and other panel members have voted, the panel Chair has a second vote, i.e. the casting vote (Guidance 1.46).
- It is important for the Chair to remind social workers and attending applicants that the panel makes a recommendation and not a decision and to give a time-frame for the agency decision.
- The panel Chair has a responsibility, with the agency adviser to the panel, to review annually the performance of all central list and panel members (Guidance 1.36).
- Linked to the review, the Chair should have a role in the appointment and induction of new central list members and in any consideration about terminating the appointment of a member.
- The Chair has a gatekeeping role in relation to papers coming to panel: 'Where there are concerns about a report, the agency adviser and the panel Chair should consider whether it is adequate for submission to panel' (Guidance 1.33).
- AAR 19(2) makes clear that 'no member of the adoption panel shall take part in any decision made by the adoption agency'. This suggests that a meeting after each panel between the Chair and the decision-maker is probably not good practice. If a meeting is needed, it may be more appropriate for the agency adviser to be involved. However, a regular meeting, perhaps every six months, to discuss general issues, could be very useful.

Other responsibilities of the Chair are likely to be:

- involvement in decisions on the attendance of observers at panel;
- involvement when a panel member declares an interest in a case;
- involvement in deciding when an extra panel may need to be convened to consider an urgent case;
- involvement in the preparation of an annual report on the panel's work.

The Chair's crucial role in chairing panel meetings and in facilitating the making of well thought through and evidenced recommendations is described in the later section, *Reaching a recommendation*.

Their shared role, with the agency adviser, in the annual review of panel members is described in the later section, *Review of panel members*.

The Chair has particular responsibilities and requires particular skills. It is likely to work best if he or she is appointed on a regular basis to chair an agency's panel and to carry out other tasks, such as the annual review of central list members. However, it would be possible for an agency to have several people on its central list who have the experience and skills needed to chair a panel.

Social work members

Regulation 3(1)(a) requires the agency to include on its central list 'one or more social workers who have at least three years' relevant post-qualifying experience'. Guidance 1.30 specifies that this should be 'in child care social work, including direct experience in adoption work'. This could involve having worked with adopters or with a child being placed for adoption. The social workers do not need to be employed by the agency.

Elected members (local authority) or director, manager or other officer of a voluntary adoption agency

There is no requirement to have someone in this role on the central list of potential panel members. However, as representatives of the corporate parent, a local authority elected member may make a valuable contribution as a central list and panel member.

Panel members in this role need to be aware of and sensitive to the potential power dynamics between themselves and social workers from that agency who may be fellow panel members or may be presenting cases to panel.

Medical adviser

Regulation 3(1)(b) requires an agency to include on its central list the medical adviser to the adoption agency (or at least one if more than one medical adviser is appointed). Although the medical adviser is not necessary for the panel to be quorate and is not required to be appointed to the panel, their presence can be very helpful and it may be a good idea if the agency has more than one medical adviser whom it can appoint to sit on a panel.

Unlike other panel members, the medical adviser also contributes to the paperwork considered by panel. He or she is required to write a summary on the child's health, which forms part of the child's permanence report (AAR 17(1)(b)), and a summary on the prospective adopter's health, which forms part of their report for panel (AAR 25(5)(b)). The medical adviser should also be consulted when the agency prepares the adoption placement report about a match for panel (Guidance 1.7). The medical adviser will be able to add verbally to their written report and to answer questions on health issues at the request of other panel members.

It is recommended in Guidance 1.8 that the agency 'make arrangements for the appointment of its medical adviser with a local Primary Care Trust's designated doctor for looked after children'.

Independent panel members

Each panel must have an independent Chair. There is no requirement for other independent panel members although if the Chair is unable to be present, there needs to be at least one independent Vice-chair or, failing that, another independent panel member. Independence is defined in the same way as for the panel Chair. Guidance 1.19 states that panels 'are intended to be multi-disciplinary bodies with a considerable element of independence from the agency'. Guidance 1.30 suggests that 'suitable members could include specialists in education, child and adolescent mental health, race and culture; and those who have personal experience of adoption'. The adoption panel has an important role in providing independent scrutiny of the work of the agency in relation to the cases presented to it. Panels as constituted up to now have benefited greatly from the rich and varied experience and expertise of their independent panel members.

It is important that people with personal experience of adoption who may join a panel have the opportunity to consider how they may feel when drawing on their own experience in reading panel papers and in panel discussion.

Vice-chair

Regulation 4(1)(b) requires the agency to appoint one or two people from the central list to be Vice-chairs. Guidance 1.30 confirms that there is no requirement for the Vice-chair to be independent of the agency 'though this would be preferable where feasible'.

The Vice-chairs are expected to have the same skills and experience as the Chair and should be given appropriate training to help them deputise for the Chair.

Agency adviser to the panel

Regulation 8 requires that:

> (1) *The adoption agency must appoint a senior member of staff, or where local authorities agree to constitute joint adoption panels as necessary, appoint a senior member of staff of one of them (referred to in this regulation as the "agency adviser"):*
> *(a) to assist the agency with the maintenance of the central list and the constitution of adoption panels;*
> *(b) to be responsible for the induction and training of persons in the central list;*
> *(c) to be responsible for liaison between*

Effective Adoption Panels

> the agency and the adoption panel, monitoring the performance of persons in the central list and members of the adoption panel and the administration of adoption panels; and
>
> (d) to give such advice to an adoption panel as the panel may request in relation to any case or generally.
>
> (2) The agency adviser must be a social worker and have at least five years' relevant post-qualifying experience and, in the opinion of the adoption agency, relevant management experience.

Guidance 1.31 states that: 'The person appointed should be someone with experience as an adoption team leader or someone who has more senior management experience and who has experience of adoption'.

The adviser 'is not a panel member and cannot take part in the decision making process. They should be able to contribute to panel meetings by raising issues and providing advice, for example, about the agency's procedures and practices' (Guidance 1.32).

Guidance adds the following:

- *The agency adviser should maintain an overview of the quality of the agency's reports to the panel and liaise with team managers to quality assure the child's permanence report, the prospective adopter's report and the adoption placement report. Where there are concerns about a report, the agency adviser and the panel Chair should consider whether it is adequate for submission to the panel.* (Guidance 1.33)
- *It is recommended that the agency adviser should also update the panel on the general progress of the cases it has considered.* (Guidance 1.34)
- *Arrangements should be made by the agency adviser to the panel for the safe keeping of the minutes and the record.* (Guidance 1.48)

The annual review of the performance of all panel members apart from the Chair is to be carried out by the agency adviser and the Chair (Guidance 1.36). This important shared duty of the agency adviser is described in more detail in the later section in the chapter, *Review of panel members*.

Legal advice

It is not a requirement for the agency's legal adviser to be a panel member and in practice very few are.

Regulations state that the panel 'must obtain legal advice in relation to the case' when considering adoption as the plan for a child (AAR 18(2)(c)). However, when considering the suitability of adopters or a match for adoption, the panel may obtain legal advice as it considers necessary in relation to the case (AAR 26(2)(c) and AAR 32(2)(c)).

Guidance 2.65 states that: 'Advice to the panel may be given orally and in writing'.

Since 2011, when children's cases moved to being considered by the ADM (except in consent cases), local authorities have reported that few legal advisers now attend the panel. It is important in these situations that there is an arrangement for the legal adviser to see the papers on cases coming to panel so that they are able to alert and inform the panel in writing about any legal issues. Equally, the panel Chair and panel members need to ensure that they raise any legal issues before the panel meeting so that if the legal adviser is not present and has not given legal advice, this does not lead to a case being deferred for legal advice.

Attendance of non-panel members at panel meetings

The agency adviser to the panel and the minute taker will be in attendance at each meeting.

Clearly, the social worker and, if possible, their manager should attend to present their case. When adoption is being considered as the plan for a child, it can be helpful for the child's foster carer to attend.

When the suitability of prospective adopters is being considered, 'Before making any recommendation, the adoption panel must invite the prospective adopters to attend a meeting of the panel' (AAR 26(4)). Guidance 3.69 states that: 'This invitation should be extended to the prospective adopter each time the panel meets to discuss their case'. Agencies should also invite prospective adopters to attend the panel which is considering their match with a particular child. Prospective adopters' attendance at panel in both these situations is discussed further in Chapters 4 and 5.

Establishing the panel

The prospective adopter may wish to bring a support person with them to panel. This is discussed further in Chapter 4.

Some panels have also, on occasion, invited a birth parent or a child or young person to attend panel. This is discussed further in Chapter 3.

NMS 23.13 requires that each person on the central list is given an opportunity to observe a panel meeting before they sit on a panel. It can be helpful for social workers who may, in future, be bringing cases to panel, to attend a panel meeting as an observer. This can also be a valuable training opportunity for doctors and lawyers. However, there should not normally be more than one or two observers at panel. Attendance should be agreed by the agency adviser to the panel, if necessary in consultation with the Chair. Observers should sign a confidentiality agreement.

It is helpful if there is a feedback questionnaire for non-panel members, particularly prospective adopters and presenting social workers, who attend panel. Information can be collated and reported back to panel to inform practice. The feedback can also contribute to the performance review of the Chair and other panel members.

Quorum

Regulation 6 specifies that: 'No business may be conducted by an adoption panel unless at least the following meet as a panel'. These are:

- the person appointed to chair the panel or one of the Vice-chairs;
- a social worker with at least three years' relevant post-qualifying experience;
- three other members or four if the panel is a joint one. If the Chair is not present and the Vice-chair who is chairing the meeting is not independent of the agency, at least one of these members must be an independent person.

All these members must, as required by Regulation 4, be drawn from people on the agency's central list.

In practice, many agencies appoint at least six or seven members to each panel. This allows for any last-minute apology and ensures that the panel is always quorate.

Appointment of substitutes

Although all members sitting as an adoption panel must be drawn from the agency's central list, Guidance 1.28 states that: 'There is no limit to the number of people who may be included on the central list'. Guidance 1.42 states that, subject to a panel being quorate, 'it is for the agency to decide how many panel members should be present at each panel meeting'. There is more discussion of this in the section on membership – practice issues.

Recruitment to the central list

Recruitment of adoption panel members has traditionally been largely through approaches to individuals based on personal recommendations. While this can work well, it can also lead to panel members being drawn from a rather narrow group of people already known to the agency.

Another method that is successfully used is direct approaches to adoption self-help groups, including Natural Parents' Network (NPN) for birth parents and Adoption UK for adoptive parents. CoramBAAF's website could also be used to advertise for central list members.

These organisations can be asked to suggest individuals or can be asked to put a request in their newsletters. The post adoption centres have also put requests for panel members in their newsletters (see Appendix IV). Some agencies have also advertised successfully in the local or national press. An internal newsletter could also be used to advertise for social worker members. Before doing this, an agency needs to be clear about what the task required is (job specification) and also what particular skills and experience they are looking for in this member (person specification). Applicants can then be short-listed and interviewed against open and clear criteria.

Sample job descriptions and person specifications for central list and panel members and Chairs are included in Appendix V.

When there is a need for new members on the central list, existing members could be involved in discussion about the particular skills and expertise that may be lacking and which a new member could provide.

Effective Adoption Panels

Central list and panel membership agreement

Guidance 1.29 specifies that: 'Before including an individual on the central list, the agency should inform them in writing of their performance objectives...The individual members should sign an acceptance form to record their agreement to these objectives.' The objectives given are:

- participation in induction and training;
- safeguarding the confidentiality of records and information submitted to the panel.

Additional points that could be included are:

- commitment to attend panel meetings as agreed with the agency;
- commitment to declare an interest and inform the Chair should a panel member have knowledge, in either a personal or professional capacity, of a case under consideration;
- commitment to anti-discriminatory practice and a preparedness to consider each case on its own merits;
- commitment to read the panel papers carefully and to come prepared to contribute to the panel discussion;
- arrival on time for panel meetings;
- willingness to consider attending an extra panel to deal with an urgent case;
- readiness to participate constructively in the annual review of their performance as a member;
- commitment to inform the agency at once if they have been charged, cautioned or convicted for any criminal offence or if any criminal proceedings are pending.

The adoption agency, for its part, should make a commitment to:

- provide induction training and written information to help prepare central list and panel members for the task, the written information to be updated as required. NMS 23.16 requires that 'each person on the central list has access to appropriate training and skills development and is kept abreast of relevant changes to legislation, regulations and guidance';
- arrange at least an annual training day for all central list and panel members;
- offer individual support and help, as far as practicable, should the member need or request this;
- undertake an annual review of the member's performance;
- send all the necessary information for each case at least five working days in advance of the date when the cases will be considered;
- assist members, if necessary, in the provision of a suitable, secure storage space for confidential panel papers while they are in the panel member's home;
- reimburse travel costs and consider the payment of a fee for reading panel papers and panel attendance;
- make available an opportunity for members to make representations or complaints to the agency;
- discuss informally any concerns about a panel member's behaviour or conduct in the panel and, if necessary, convene an additional review. If these concerns cannot be resolved, the agency will put in writing the reasons why it is ending the member's appointment to the central list.

There should be a central list and panel membership agreement that sets out these mutual commitments of the adoption panel member and the agency. It should be signed by the central list member and by a representative of the agency. This could be the agency adviser or the agency decision-maker. It would be helpful to have a specific agreement for the Chair. Suggested formats for this are included in Appendix V.

Checks on central list and panel members

These apply to everyone on the agency's central list. They are listed in NMS 21.3. Every applicant must be interviewed and a record must be maintained of:

- identity checks;
- criminal records check from the Disclosure and Barring Service (DBS);
- checks to confirm qualifications;
- at least two references, with written references verified by telephone;
- checks to confirm the right to work in the UK;
- where the person has lived outside the UK, further checks considered appropriate to supplement the DBS check.

Establishing the panel

All social workers and others working with children are required to have DBS checks. Although panel members will not usually have direct contact with children, they do receive comprehensive information on vulnerable children which could put children at risk if misused. Their check is the lower level enhanced check. There is no longer a requirement in regulations or statutory guidance for panel members to renew their DBS checks and so it is a matter for the adoption agency to determine, as part of their agency's policy, whether they will renew these checks and with what frequency.

Where an agency decides to renew DBS checks, every three years could be seen as reasonable and good practice. The DBS Update Service (www.gov.uk/dbs-update-service) allows agencies to check online whether there have been any changes to a panel member's DBS record. There is a subscription cost to this service paid by the applicant (currently £13 a year) but not to the agency making the check, but this can be useful to panel members who have other roles where a DBS is required.

Prospective central list members will be asked to supply the names of at least two people who can give a reference as to their suitability as a panel member. Telephone enquiries will be made to each referee to verify the written reference (NMS 21.1). There will also be discussion with the member about the professional and/or personal qualifications and experience that will inform their contribution to the panel. The agency will require evidence of qualifications and experience. Proof of identity, including a recent photograph, will be required.

Induction and training

NMS 23.13–16 specifies that:

- *The adoption agency provides each person on the central list with an opportunity of observing an adoption panel before they sit on an adoption panel.*
- *Each person on the central list is given induction training which is completed within 10 weeks of being included on the central list.*
- *Each person on the central list is given the opportunity of attending an annual joint training day with the agency's adoption staff.*
- *Each person on the central list has access to appropriate training and skills development and is kept abreast of relevant changes to legislation, regulation and guidance.*

It is important that central list and panel members are adequately prepared and trained for the job they do. Members should discuss their training needs at the annual review of their panel performance (see section on this) but should also raise issues and ask for information or help at any stage. The agency adviser and the panel Chair are the appropriate people to ask.

Members should be offered and should attend at least one day's training a year. Joint training with, for instance, members of the adoption team and with representatives from child care teams, on issues of common concern can be helpful. This can also be an opportunity for constructive feedback on how each group is perceived by the other.

It can also be helpful for members to have the opportunity for some training on working as a member of an adoption panel.

CoramBAAF provides training in relation to adoption panel membership and for adoption and child care workers (see Appendix IV).

Review of central list and panel members

Central list and panel members must be given written information on what will be expected of them and also what they can expect from the agency, before they are appointed. This is detailed in the sections, *Central list and panel membership agreement* and *Induction and training*.

There is a requirement that there should be an annual review of each central list and panel member's performance. This will be conducted by the agency adviser to the panel and the panel Chair. The Chair's performance review will be conducted by the agency's decision-maker (Guidance 1.36). Suggested formats are included in the appendices.

Each member's performance will be reviewed against the written objectives agreed with them before their appointment. The review could provide a useful opportunity for a panel member to talk about any issues that may have inhibited his or her performance. These could include, for instance, a panel process that allows forceful or voluble panel members always

Effective Adoption Panels

to get in first with issues and questions or an agenda that is so tight that there is inadequate time for all panel members to contribute. It will also provide an opportunity for constructive feedback by the panel Chair and agency adviser on the panel member's contribution to panel meetings. It would be helpful if this could be evidenced by feedback from the other panel members and from presenting social workers and applicants who have attended panel. The need for further input or training could be agreed and arrangements made to provide this.

If, in that year, a person has never been invited to sit on a panel, they and the agency may decide that they should come off the list. It will clearly be difficult to review the performance of a member who has only sat on a panel a few times, or not at all. The member may wish to query how and by whom decisions are made to appoint people to a panel and the reasons why he or she has rarely or never been appointed.

The Chair's performance is reviewed by the agency's decision-maker, who may need to attend some panel meetings as an observer, to enable him or her to do the review. He or she should also seek views about the Chair's performance from other panel members, and from social workers and prospective adopters who attend panel (Guidance 1.36).

Brief feedback sheets for presenting social workers and prospective adopters who attend panel on the process as a whole, the role of the Chair and the contribution of any individual panel members are likely to be helpful. It might also be worth considering a form for panel members to use to make comments on the panel as a whole, on the Chair's contribution and on any other particular dynamics or issues.

Some agencies use a group approach for reviews. All central list members gather for half a day. Each writes positive comments and suggestions for change about other central list members on post-its that are put onto a flipchart for each person. These are then considered and reflected on, with feedback to the group. A form, similar to the one in Appendix V, is then completed. The Chair is part of the process but has an individual review.

Adoption panel fees

A local authority may pay to any member of an adoption panel constituted by it such fee as it may determine, being a fee of a reasonable amount. (Regulation 4(4))

Guidance 1.39 states that a voluntary adoption agency may also pay a fee to any member of its adoption panel.

Guidance 1.40 states that fees could either be for each panel attended or paid as an annual amount. Fees can cover preparation time as well as attendance at panel and expenses can also be paid for travel to and from panel meetings and related activities.

Many adoption agencies already pay fees to panel members. This enables them to recruit a wider range of panel members, not just those whose employer is prepared to donate their time or who can afford to give time on a voluntary basis. The Chair has a wider range of responsibilities than other panel members and will usually be paid a higher fee.

Tenure of office of members of the central list and adoption panel

There is no requirement in regulations about tenure. However, there is nothing to prevent an agency from appointing people to its central list for a set period if it wishes. This would need to be set out clearly in the panel membership agreement, 'a signed document which sets out the mutual commitments of those individuals on the central list and the agency' – Guidance 1.3. Guidance 1.36 requires each panel member's performance to be reviewed annually and this could be an opportunity to extend an agreed period of appointment if both the agency and the member agree. The agency will need to balance the need for some consistency with the need for new recruits to the central list from time to time.

Resignation by central list and panel members

A person who is included in the central list may at any time ask to be removed from the central list by giving one month's notice in writing. (Regulation 3(2))

Any adoption panel member may resign at any time by giving one month's notice in writing to the adoption agency which appointed them. (Regulation 4(5))

Obviously, it is helpful if members can give more notice than this if possible, to enable a replacement member to be recruited.

Termination of appointment of central list and panel members

Where the adoption agency is of the opinion that a person included in the central list is unsuitable or unable to remain in the list the agency may remove that person's name from the list by giving them one month's notice in writing with reasons. (Regulation 3(3))

Guidance 1.37 states that:

Where an agency identifies that the chair or an individual on the central list is not performing to the required standard, perhaps as part of the review process, it should ensure that this is discussed promptly with the individual with the aim of addressing any developmental needs through advice and training.

Even if a review is not due, the agency adviser and the panel Chair might want to consider setting one up so that there can be a structured discussion with the member about their below standard performance. This might follow an informal discussion by the panel Chair and/or panel adviser with the member to try to resolve the problem. If it is the Chair whose performance is of concern, the agency decision-maker would need to be involved for further discussion and possibly for a formal review.

Where an adoption agency is of the opinion that any member of the adoption panel appointed by it is unsuitable or unable to continue as a panel member, it may terminate that member's appointment at any time by giving the member notice in writing with reasons. (Regulation 4(6))

Guidance 1.38 clarifies that this may arise, for example, 'when a previously unidentified conflict of interest arises (e.g. the individual knows the prospective adopters), etc.' The individual's appointment to that particular panel would be terminated but they would remain on the central list.

Adoption panel functions

The adoption panel has three key functions in relation to children and families. It must consider:

- *The case of every child referred to it by the adoption agency and make a recommendation to the agency as to whether the child should be placed for adoption.* (AAR 18(1))

These will be children whose birth parents are consenting to their adoption. It must also consider, and may give advice to the agency about:

(a) *the arrangements which the agency proposes to make for allowing any person contact with the child; and*

(b) *where the agency is a local authority, whether an application should be made by the authority for a placement order in respect of the child.* (AAR 18(3))

- *The case of the prospective adopter referred to it by the adoption agency and make a recommendation to the agency as to whether the prospective adopter is suitable to adopt a child.* (AAR 26(1))

It may also consider and give advice to the agency about the number of children the prospective adopter may be suitable to adopt, their age range, sex, likely needs and background (AAR 26(3)).

- *The proposed placement referred to it by the adoption agency and make a recommendation to the agency as to whether the child should be placed for adoption with that particular prospective adopter.* (AAR 32(1))

It must also consider and may give advice to the agency about:

(a) *...the authority's proposal for the provision of adoption support services for the adoptive family;*

(b) *the arrangements the adoption agency proposes to make for allowing any person contact with the child; and*

(c) *whether the parental responsibility of any parent or guardian or the prospective adopter should be restricted and, if so, the extent of any such restriction.* (AAR 32(3))

These three functions are described in more detail in Chapters 3, 4, 5 and 6.

- Another key function of the panel is in relation to policies and procedures. The adoption agency must have 'written policy and procedural instructions governing the functioning of the agency and an adoption panel', and such persons in the central list as the agency considers appropriate must be consulted about these (Regulation 7).

- Guidance 1.19 states that: 'Panels play an important quality assurance role providing objectivity and having the ability to challenge practice which is felt not to be in the interests of children or fall short of the Regulations or NMS. Panels are required to give regular feedback to the agency.'

This is described in more detail in Chapter 2.

Adoption and permanence panel and concurrent planning and Fostering for Adoption (FFA)

The consideration of the suitability of foster carers must be done by a panel that complies with the Fostering Services Regulations 2011. Fostering plans for children and matches for long-term fostering are not required to be considered by a panel and so there are no regulatory requirements. However, Guidance 1.24 states that:

Given the significance of long-term fostering, many agencies have established adoption and permanence panels, which combine knowledge and experience of adoption and fostering, and enable these two permanence options to be considered by one panel.

This was particularly helpful when panels were considering permanent plans for older children, which could be either adoption or long-term fostering. However, this will happen very rarely now given that there will be court scrutiny of the majority of these plans and they will therefore not be considered by the panel.

Agencies could continue to involve the panel in considering long-term fostering plans but may choose not to do so, given that the panel is no longer considering an adoption plan for the majority of children. An adoption and permanence panel could still be involved in considering long-term fostering matches.

Concurrency planning involves carers who have dual approval as foster carers under the fostering regulations and as prospective adopters under adoption regulations. A child, usually a baby or toddler, can then be placed on a fostering basis while work with birth parents is attempted. If this is not successful, the child, after necessary court and panel involvement, can remain and be adopted by their foster carers. Borthwick and Donnelly (2013) state that 'experience suggests that the model of adoption and permanence panels is the most effective' for this dual approval as foster carers and adopters. However, 'it is important for the agency decision-maker, Chair and central list panel members to be briefed, trained and supported in the specific issues that might arise in concurrent planning.' The panel will need to be compliant with fostering and adoption regulations and make effective use of the central list.

Fostering for Adoption (FFA) was initially introduced by regulations in 2013 and was then developed and included in the provisions of the Children and Families Act 2014. It is discussed further in Chapter 4.

The 2014 Act introduced a new duty on local authorities, under s.22C(9A) of the Children Act 1989, to consider placing a looked after child, for whom the local authority is considering adoption, with foster carers who are also approved prospective adopters following consideration in accordance with s.22C(9B)(c). The FFA carers may be dually approved as foster carers at the same time as being approved as adopters under the Fostering Services (England) Regulations 2011, as they are in concurrent planning schemes or they may be approved as temporary foster carers for a named child under Regulation 25A of the Care Planning, Placement and Case Review (England) Regulations 2010 (the 2010 Regulations). In these cases their temporary approval is agreed by a Nominated Officer and they are not presented to panel for approval.

Statutory guidance on early permanence placements and approval of prospective adopters as foster carers (July 2014) sets out guidance for local authorities about these placements, and further practice guidance on FFA was also published by Coram and BAAF in 2013. (This guidance will be updated by CoramBAAF in 2017 as a Good Practice Guide.)

FFA is used for children where the local authority has decided that the plan for the child should be adoption, and has identified that there are no suitable family members but they are still seeking a placement order.

However, Practice Guidance on FFA states that:

If an agency wishes to have some adopters also approved as foster carers in this way, before a specific child has been identified for placement, an adoption and permanence panel able to consider both approvals would be likely to work best.

Adoption reports

The key social work reports received by the panel are:

- the child's permanence report (CPR);
- the prospective adopter's report (PAR); and
- the adoption placement report (APR).

These are required by regulation to be completed by workers who either have the necessary qualifications and experience or are supervised by someone who does. Social workers employed by the agency should have at least three years' post-qualifying experience in childcare social work, including direct experience of adoption work. This would include work with adoptive families or work in placing a child for adoption. If the social worker (or student) does not have this experience, they must be supervised by someone who does. An independent social worker, acting on behalf of the agency, must have the necessary experience and be supervised by someone who does (The Restriction on the Preparation of Adoption Reports Regulations (ARR) 2005).

Guidance 1.15 clarifies that it is not necessary for the supervised social worker to be under the direct line management of the supervising social worker.

Where reports are being completed by workers without the necessary experience, 'the draft report should be considered and discussed during supervision and signed off by a social worker with the necessary experience before the report is submitted to the adoption panel' (Guidance 1.16). It is likely to be helpful both for the inexperienced worker and for panel members if the supervising social worker can attend panel as well. The agency adviser to the panel could be asked to ensure that this happens.

Regulations specifically require the panel to consider all the information and reports passed to it by the agency. Where the panel considers that additional information is needed in relation to any of its three key functions, it may ask for this and the agency 'must obtain, so far as is reasonably practicable, any other relevant information which may be required by the adoption panel and send that information to the panel' (AAR 17(3), 25(10), 31(5)).

Declaring an interest

Panel members who have had any involvement in a case to be considered, or who know any of the people involved, should declare an interest and should say whether they think this will prejudice their consideration of the case. If they do, they should not participate in that case, and it is probably best if they leave the room. If the panel member does not feel their knowledge will affect their consideration of the case, it will be the responsibility of the Chair, possibly with the help of the legal adviser, to make a final decision. It is important for panel members to alert the agency adviser or panel Chair as early as possible before the panel to avoid a possible problem over quoracy.

Reaching a recommendation

- Panel members must consider cases referred to them and make a recommendation to the agency.
- They must consider and take into account the reports sent to them.
- They may request the agency to obtain any further relevant information that they consider necessary.
- When considering the plan for a child they must obtain legal advice. When considering the suitability of adopters or a match they may do so.
- Panels can only make recommendations when they are quorate.
- Panels can make
  - a positive recommendation; or
  - a negative recommendation; or
  - defer making a recommendation until they have further specific information to enable them to do so.
- Although the Guidance makes no explicit reference to not making "in principle" recommendations, it makes clear that the decision-maker's decision must be based on a definite recommendation.

The panel Chair has a very important role. He or she should ensure that each panel member has an opportunity to ask questions or make comments on every issue. This may be facilitated by asking each member in turn for their questions and comments, starting with a different person each time. Each panel member should be asked whether he or she supports a proposed recommendation. Guidance 1.46 makes clear that: 'Where panel members have serious reservations, the panel Chair must ensure that these are recorded in the minutes and are attached to the panel's recommendations'. Guidance 1.46 further states that: 'If the panel cannot reach a consensus on its recommendation, after the chair and other members of the panel have voted, the panel chair has a second vote, i.e. the casting vote'. It will probably be helpful to both panel members and to the minute taker if the Chair summarises each recommendation made and the reasons for it, as well as any dissenting views, with reasons, during the meeting. This will ensure, as far as possible, that an accurate record is made.

Many cases are very complex, with risk factors as well as positive factors in relation to the issue for recommendation. It is important that there is rigorous consideration of the written information presented, and that relevant questions are asked of presenting social workers and of applicants, and their answers carefully considered. Many panels take time to formulate their issues and questions before presenting social workers and applicants are invited in to panel. Many panels also ask applicants and, less frequently, presenting social workers, to leave while they formulate their recommendation.

If panel members cannot reach a recommendation because important and relevant information is not available, they should defer making a recommendation. It should be made clear to the presenting social workers what additional information is needed, the realistic possibility of obtaining this should be discussed and a date should be set, if at all possible, for the case to come back to panel.

It is, however, important that deferring making a recommendation is not in fact an excuse for not coming to a conclusion when information is available. There may be gaps but there may be clear reasons for these, e.g. information about a father whom a mother is unable to name or adamantly refuses to name. All panel members should work hard to reach a view. Abstentions are not appropriate or helpful. No recommendation is likely to be risk free, and making a negative recommendation may result in a child drifting in the system, without a clear plan or without an adoptive family. However, it will sometimes be necessary, with the child's welfare always as the paramount consideration, to make a recommendation that a proposed plan, approval of a family or a match should not go ahead.

The decision-maker

Guidance 1.52 states that the decision-maker is a senior person within the adoption agency. VAAs may also appoint a trustee or director. This Guidance also states that 'there may be more than one decision-maker in an agency. The decision-maker may not delegate their authority to another person.' Agencies should therefore generally have at least two named and appropriately qualified decision-makers to ensure cover for any absence of one of them. Guidance 1.50 states that the decision-maker 'does not have direct management responsibility for the adoption panel'. NMS 23.17 requires that the decision-maker 'is a social worker with at least three years' post qualifying experience in child care social work and has knowledge and experience of permanency planning for children, adoption and child care law and practice'. In addition, where the adoption agency provides an intercountry adoption service, the decision-maker should have a good knowledge of intercountry adoption legislation and practice.

Agency decision-making

The Regulations ensure that the panel has a separate identity from the agency, and is independent of it. The agency cannot delegate decision-making to the panel. However, it is required to refer certain matters to the panel (see section on *Adoption panel functions*) and to take its recommendations into consideration before making decisions on these matters.

Regulations in relation to the three key functions of panel make it clear that 'no member of the adoption panel shall take part in any decision made by the adoption agency' (AAR 19(2), AAR 27(2), AAR 33(2)). The decision-maker may, however, discuss the case with the agency adviser, medical issues with the medical adviser, and seek legal advice if they wish (Guidance 1.55 and 1.56). These discussions must be recorded in the child's and/or prospective adopter's care file. Guidance 1.53 and 1.54 further set out guidance from a court case in 2009 about the way in which the decision-maker should approach a case. They must have a final set of panel minutes and should 'ask whether they agree with the process and approach of the relevant panel(s) and are satisfied as to its fairness and that the panel has properly addressed the arguments'.

Guidance 1.57 states that the decision-maker must reach a decision within seven working days of

Establishing the panel

receiving the panel's recommendation and final set of minutes, or of receiving reports (i.e. in a case where the panel is not involved).

Guidance makes it clear that, where the panel has provided the agency with advice, for example, about the range of approval for prospective adopters and about proposed adoption support services, contact arrangements and the exercise of parental responsibility in relation to a match, the agency decision-maker may 'express a view on such advice'. The local authority must make a decision about adoption support services, contact arrangements and the exercise of parental responsibility. These decisions may be taken by the senior manager who is the agency decision-maker or by another manager (Guidance 2.67, 3.73 and 4.35).

It is important that, in drawing up its procedures, the agency ensures that a satisfactory means of communication is established between the agency decision-maker and the panel. If, for example, the decision-maker were repeatedly to refuse to accept the panel's recommendations, it would be necessary to have an arrangement whereby differing views could be explored. It may be helpful for the decision-maker to attend the panel as an observer occasionally (provided that he or she takes no part in proceedings or discussion). They may usefully also attend at least part of a training day with panel members.

Administration

Good administrative arrangements are essential for the effective functioning of a panel. Responsibility for the administration of the panel is given by Regulation 8 to the agency adviser to the panel. He or she should ensure that sufficient administrative support is provided for the efficient performance of the tasks listed below. Any necessary training should be provided for the staff concerned.

The agency should, in consultation with central list members, determine the frequency and usual length of meetings and the number of cases to be considered at each. Many panels allocate about 45 minutes for consideration of a child's plan or the suitability of prospective adopters and perhaps an hour for consideration of a match.

There should also be a decision about whether or not forms need anonymising. Some agencies do this while others do not, and there are pros and cons of both practices.

Main administrative functions

Before panel meetings:

- Production of an annual schedule of meetings.

- Maintenance of a panel booking system.

- Notification to social workers of panel schedule and deadlines. Arrangement of accommodation and refreshments for meetings with, and if practicable, a private waiting area for, applicants and others attending the meeting.

- Preparation of agendas.

- Maintenance of records of central list members, confidentiality agreements, etc.

- Working with the agency adviser, liaison with social workers and managers as required to ensure that the panel's requirements are met. This should include ensuring that social workers submit reports in good time, in the quantity required and in conformity with the panel's requirements.

- Responding to enquiries from social workers about appearances before the panel, panel procedures and reporting requirements.

- Receiving of reports and bringing to the attention of the agency adviser any apparent gap.

- Ensuring that appropriate members and numbers are able to attend meetings to ensure a quorum.

- Liaison with the Chair about requests in relation to observers.

- Arranging for the copying and collating of papers and ensuring that they are sent out securely packaged to panel members.

- NMS 17.4 requires that 'all necessary information is provided to panel members at least five working days in advance of the panel meeting to enable full and proper consideration'.

- Ensuring that meeting and waiting rooms are prepared for the meeting, that name plates/badges are ready, that spare reports are available, that refreshments are ready, that recording equipment if used is functioning, etc.

At the meeting:

- Taking minutes, noting in particular, recommendations made and reasons given.
- Drawing to the attention of the Chair any matters requiring his or her attention.
- Collection of papers at end of the meeting.

After the meeting:

- Drafting minutes, including recommendations made and reasons given.
- Submitting draft minutes to the Chair or agency adviser as appropriate for checking and to panel members for ratification.
- Ensuring that the agency decision-maker receives the agreed minutes and any other papers required for the decision to be made.
- Ensuring that applicants, the child's parents or guardian and social workers are notified in writing of decisions.
- Providing the social worker with relevant minutes.
- Maintaining full records of panel business, including agenda, reports and minutes.
- Maintaining records for performance monitoring, government returns and the annual report.

Minutes

An adoption panel must make a written record of its proceedings, its recommendations and the reasons for its recommendations. (Regulation 6(2))

Guidance 1.45 specifies that:

The panel chair is responsible for ensuring the accuracy of the panel's recommendations, reasons and, following agreement with panel members, the minutes. The chair must also make sure that a person who is not a member of the panel fulfils the task of writing these documents.

Good minuting of panel meetings is essential. Guidance 1.46 states that:

It is important that the panel minutes carefully record the names of panel members attending the meeting, and the names and roles of any other people present at the meeting. The minutes must accurately reflect the discussion and cover the key issues rather than be a verbatim record of the meeting. Where panel members have serious reservations, the panel chair must ensure these are recorded in the minutes and are attached to the panel's recommendation... The panel's minutes should clearly set out the reasons why the chair had to use the casting vote.

NMS 17.11 requires that the decision-maker makes a decision 'within seven working days of receipt of the recommendation and final set of panel minutes'.

The panel Chair will usually check draft minutes but all panel members need to check and agree draft minutes before they are sent to the decision-maker. Many agencies email draft minutes to panel members within a day or two of the panel meeting, requesting speedy comments.

Guidance 1.54 further requires that the agency decision-maker must consider the minutes of the panel meeting, as well as all the reports submitted.

Minutes of the panel's consideration of adoption as the plan for the child and of a match should be put on the child's case record (AAR 12, 33). Minutes of the panel's consideration of the suitability of prospective adopters should be put on their case record (AAR 22).

CoramBAAF has produced a useful pamphlet titled *A Guide to Writing Panel Minutes* (Pratt, 2016).

Disclosure of minutes

The agency has discretion to share minutes if it decides that this would be appropriate and helpful. However, the Adoption and Children Act 2002 (Consequential Amendments) Order 2005 amends the Data Protection (Miscellaneous Subject Access Exemptions) Order 2000 to provide for exemption from the right of access in respect of adoption records and reports.

Agencies should consider with their legal adviser whether or not to agree to disclosure. A principle of the Data Protection Act (DPA), which could be kept in mind when making this decision, is whether the disclosure of information would identify another individual who has not consented to its disclosure. This could include, for example, information in the minutes about comments made by personal referees.

There is also an exemption in the DPA that extends to all social work records and which could be kept in mind. This provides that data need not be disclosed if doing so will be likely to prejudice the carrying out of social work by causing serious harm to the physical or mental health or condition of the data subject or another person. This means, for example, that an agency could refuse access to minutes to a birth parent if there was a serious risk that the anger this might induce in the parent might lead to an attack on a child, another parent or anyone else. Agencies should consider with their legal adviser whether or not to agree to disclosure.

Courts can order minutes to be disclosed as part of proceedings. A child's guardian in proceedings is entitled to see the child's case record, which will contain minutes of a panel that has considered a plan or match for the child.

Electronic communication

A few agencies are starting to issue papers and circulate minutes electronically for members to view on computers but also on mobile devices. It will be essential that central list members are fully briefed and trained on confidentiality and security issues, and provided with appropriate equipment as necessary.

Monitoring and review

It is recommended in Guidance 1.34 that the agency adviser should update the panel on the general progress of the cases it has considered. This could be in the form of three- or six-monthly reports on any children and families considered since the last report, on children waiting for placement and also in placement but not yet adopted, and on waiting approved families.

It is also important that some time is set aside regularly for general issues to be raised by panel members or by the panel adviser. Some of these might need fuller discussion at subsequent panel training.

Guidance 1.19 states that: 'Panels play an important quality assurance role, providing objectivity and having the ability to challenge practice which is felt not to be in the interests of children or to fall short of the Regulations or NMS'.

NMS 17.2 requires that: '... adoption panels provide a quality assurance feedback to the agency every six months on the quality of reports being presented to the panel'. It will probably be helpful for the panel to note at the end of each panel, perhaps in a log kept by the Chair, any quality assurance issues which may have arisen. Some of these may need to be taken up with the agency straight away but they should also be noted for inclusion in the six-monthly report. NMS 22.8 specifies that the adoption panel which dealt with the case is informed of any subsequent allegations made against a prospective adopter or member of the prospective adopters' household and of the outcome of investigations into the allegation.

Review of panel work

It is good practice for a brief annual report of panel activities to be produced. This could include information about membership, statistics, an account of activities and information on key issues of interest and concern. This report could help central list members to be informed and involved in the work of panels. If such a report were to be circulated, it could help to integrate the work of the panel into the wider work of the agency.

Adoption inspection

Ofsted is the organisation responsible for inspecting adoption services every three years. (They also inspect fostering services annually.) An inspector may want to observe a panel meeting as part of the inspection, and will interview the Chair and possibly other panel members too. Panel members should ensure that they receive the conclusions of the inspectors, both about the panel and also about the adoption service in general.

In June/July 2013, Ofsted consulted about introducing a single framework for inspecting services for all vulnerable children. Services for the health, protection and care of children, including arrangements for local authority fostering and adoption services, would be inspected together, thereby offering an integrated overview. Consultation on Good Voluntary Adoption Provision was carried out at the same time.

References

Borthwick S and Donnelly S (2013) *Concurrent Planning: Achieving early permanence for babies and young children*, London: BAAF

Coram and BAAF (2013) *Fostering for Adoption Practice Guidance*, London: Coram and BAAF, available at: www.corambaaf.org.uk/webfm_send/3217

Pratt J (2016) *Taking Minutes at Panel Meetings*, London: CoramBAAF

2 Agency policy and practice issues

Making the adoption process work well

There is a section in the introduction to the Guidance – para 5, 'Making the adoption process work well' – which is included here, in brief.

Experience and research have identified the factors that can make the adoption process work well for the child, birth parents and adoptive parents. They are, in summary:

- Actively promote adoption. A clear care planning process that always considers adoption as a possible permanence option.

- Encourage people to come forward to adopt.

- Avoid delay in the adoption process, including starting the family-finding process as soon as adoption becomes the plan following a statutory review.

- Take the fullest account of the views and wishes of the child.

- Place a child with a prospective adopter who can meet all, or most, of the child's identified needs.

- Provide an effective adoption support service.

- Collaborate effectively with the local authority's other social services and with voluntary adoption agencies.

- Develop and sustain constructive links between adoption and looked after children's teams and the courts.

- Have a practical and balanced understanding of the circumstances in which special guardianship may be more appropriate than adoption and how to manage the different processes and legal requirements.

Duties in relation to adoption

Local authorities have a legal duty under Section 3 of the Adoption and Children Act 2002 to:

Maintain within their area a service designed to meet the needs, in relation to adoption, of –

(a) children who may be adopted,

(b) parents and guardians wishing to adopt a child,

(c) adopted persons, their parents, natural parents and former guardians,

and for that purpose to provide the requisite facilities.

Local authorities can arrange for registered adoption societies, or in some cases others, to provide services on their behalf. The services to be provided include arrangements for the provision of adoption support services and an intercountry adoption service.

The "welfare checklist" in relation to adoption

Section 1 of the Adoption and Children Act 2002 details an important "checklist" which applies:

(1) ... whenever a court or adoption agency is coming to a decision relating to the adoption of a child.

(2) The paramount consideration of the court or adoption agency must be the child's welfare, throughout his life.

(3) The court or adoption agency must at all times bear in mind that, in general, any delay in coming to a decision is likely to prejudice the child's welfare.

(4) The court or adoption agency must have regard to the following matters (among others) –

(a) the child's ascertainable wishes and feelings regarding the decision (considered in the light of the child's age and understanding),

(b) the child's particular needs,

(c) the likely effect on the child (throughout his life) of having ceased to be a member of the original family and become an adopted person,

(d) the child's age, sex, background and any of the child's characteristics which the court or agency considers relevant,

(e) any harm (within the meaning of the Children Act 1989 (c.41)) which the child has suffered or is at risk of suffering,

(f) the relationship which the child has with relatives, and with any other person in relation to whom the court or agency considers the relationship to be relevant, including –

(i) the likelihood of any such relationship continuing and the value to the child of its doing so,

Agency policy and practice issues

    (ii) the ability and willingness of any of the child's relatives, or of any such person, to provide the child with a secure environment in which the child can develop, and otherwise to meet the child's needs,

    (iii) the wishes and feelings of any of the child's relatives, or of any such person, regarding the child.

(5) In placing the child for adoption, the adoption agency must give due consideration to the child's religious persuasion, racial origin and cultural and linguistic background.

(6) The court or adoption agency must always consider the whole range of powers available to it in the child's case (whether under this Act or the Children Act 1989); and the court must not make any order under this Act unless it considers that making the order would be better for the child than not doing so.

It is important for panel members to note that, for the purposes of this "checklist", references to "relationships" are not confined to legal relationships and references to a "relative", in relation to the child, include the child's mother and father.

The 2014 Act repealed the requirement to give due consideration to the child's religious persuasion, racial origin and cultural and linguistic background ethnicity in England but not in Wales. The draft Statutory Guidance 2014, sections 3.4–3.14, sets out how this should impact on the choice of placements for children and is covered later in this chapter.

It is crucial that this "checklist" is kept in mind by panel members in their consideration of every case.

Adoption is the plan for relatively few children. Statistics (DfE, 2012) indicate that just over four per cent of children looked after by English local authorities are placed for adoption, although there are wide variations between authorities. Roughly three-quarters of all children currently adopted in England and Wales have been looked after prior to adoption, most of the remaining quarter being adopted by step-parents or relatives; 4,690 looked after children were adopted in England in the year ending 31 March 2016.

However, it is extremely important that good quality adoption services are available and that adoption is a well-recognised placement option for children. 'We know that in the vast majority of cases adoption works. Education and health outcomes are as good as for children growing up with their birth parents' (foreword to the Adoption Guidance).

Social workers and their managers, panel members and service users need good quality written information on adoption arrangements, policies and procedures and these need to be regularly reviewed.

This chapter describes some of the ways of achieving good policies and practice in adoption work and some of the issues that will need to be considered by agencies and panels. It is not an exhaustive list and panel members may well need to discuss other general issues with the agency.

Achieving good policies and practice in adoption work

Children's services plans

Adoption needs to be set in the general framework of the local authority's services for children. Local authorities are required to draw up and publish a plan of the services that they offer to children and their families and this should include details of their adoption services. It may be helpful for an extract from the plan to be included in the pocket on the back cover.

Child care policy

All children need the opportunity to experience permanence within their birth family or within a new family. Many agencies have a child care policy about planning for children's permanence needs within clear timescales to prevent drift. This might include the panel's role in reviewing children identified as needing a permanent new family but still waiting. If the agency has a written child care policy, this should be included in the pocket on the back cover.

Equal opportunities/diversity policy

If the agency has an equal opportunities or diversity policy, it will underpin the work of the panel. Panel members need to be aware of their individual attitudes and prejudices and also of the way that organisational processes can lead to unfair discrimination. However, it should be remembered that the overriding principle in adoption work is the duty to give paramount consideration to the welfare of the child. It will be useful for the equal opportunities policy to be included in the pocket on the back cover.

Child protection policy

The agency will have a child protection policy and procedures and it might be helpful for some information on these to be included in the pocket on the back cover.

Adoption panel policies and procedures

NMS 17.1 requires that:

The adoption agency implements clear written policies and procedures on the recruitment to and maintenance of the central list of persons considered by them to be suitable to be members of an adoption panel ('the central list') and constitution of the adoption panel.

Guidance 1.3 recommends that the following are included in the policy and procedures document for the adoption panel.

- Details of recruitment, induction, training and performance review of those individuals on the central list.
- A signed document that sets out the mutual commitment of those individuals on the central list and the agency.
- Arrangements for informing the prospective adopter, the birth parents and, where appropriate, the child, of the panel's recommendations.
- Details of how a panel will monitor and report on its work to the agency and others.
- Arrangements and timescales for passing the panel's recommendations and minutes to the decision-maker.

It could also include information on how the agency will decide whom to invite from the central list to sit on a particular panel. Who will make this decision? Will the agency aim to have a certain number of independent members at each panel meeting? Will it aim to have more members than the minimum quorum?

The panel's involvement in contributing to good practice

An adoption agency must, in consultation with such persons in the central list as the agency considers appropriate and...with the agency's medical adviser, prepare and implement written policy and procedural instructions governing the exercise of the functions of the agency and an adoption panel in relation to adoption and such instructions shall be kept under review and, where appropriate, revised by the agency. (Regulation 7)

The medical adviser must be consulted about arrangements for access to, and disclosure of, health information. Members should discuss with the Chair and the agency adviser how they can best be involved in this consultation. Some time at a training session could be set aside for comments on a draft set of policies and procedures. Central list members, as well as staff, should be given a copy of these policy and procedures documents.

In addition to this statutory involvement, panels have the potential to make an influential contribution to good practice. Panel members should recognise and feel confident about the important role that they can play. They should always question things which are not clear or which seem inappropriate and should ask for additional information if necessary. It is also important that some time is set aside regularly for general issues to be raised.

Central list and panel members should receive regular reports of the work of the adoption agency. This should include regular, perhaps three-monthly, brief reports on the circumstances of children and adoptive applicants awaiting placement and of children placed but not yet adopted. Unfortunately, not all placements will work out successfully. Members should be notified of any placements that have disrupted. Useful insights can be gained when panel members consider placements that have disrupted. It can be a good use of time if the panel considers the original reports as well as a report into what subsequently happened.

Specific issues that panel members will need to consider

The agency may have a formal policy agreed by committee or a clear view on some of the issues identified in this section. Central list members should be consulted as appropriate by the agency (see above) in the drawing up of written policies and procedures for adoption work and in reviewing these and should therefore be broadly in agreement with them. However, the panel is independent of the agency and panel members have a responsibility to consider each individual case carefully on its own merits.

There is no such thing as the "perfect" family or the "ideal" match. Panel members need to bear in mind that no recommendation that they make is free of risk. Strengths and limitations have to be identified and weighed and extra help and support specified to address gaps. Not making positive recommendations about the plan for a child, the approval of a family or the matching of a child may mean that a child waits longer in the care system and this could be a greater risk for them. However, panel members should also be clear that, with the child's welfare as their paramount consideration, it will sometimes be necessary to reach a view that a family or a match should not be recommended.

Family structures

- **Single parents.** Guidance 4.9 states that: 'Single prospective adopters of both genders can have much to offer an adopted child. They may be able to focus all their time on meeting a child's needs and have a good level of physical and emotional availability. Some children may find it easier to relate to just one parent or prefer not to relate closely to a mother or a father figure if there are negative associations from the past. Issues of emotional and financial support, health and future close relationships will need to be carefully explored with single prospective adopters.'

- **Child's position in the family.** It is most usual for children to enter their new family as the youngest child. However, placement as the eldest or middle child can be appropriate. It is important to know what position the child has held in the past to assess whether continuing or changing this may be the most appropriate for this particular child. The wishes and feelings of existing children in the family are also obviously crucial.

- **Age gaps between children.** Research (Sellick *et al*, 2004) shows that there is a higher risk of a placement not working out if a child is placed in a family which has other children close to them in age.

- **Divorce or previously failed partnerships.** Panel members need to assess whether this is a pattern that could be repeated in the future. When there has been joint parenting experience with a previous partner, it is important to try and get the previous partner's view on how this worked. This issue is discussed in more detail in Chapter 4.

- **Unmarried partners can apply jointly for an adoption order.** Since 2005, unmarried partners have been able to apply jointly for an adoption order although unmarried couples – lesbian, gay or heterosexual – have been assessed as adopters and have had children placed with them prior to that time.

- **A big age difference between two partners.** Practice has shown that people who are comfortable with difference can be very effective parents for children with special needs. However, see also the paragraph on age in *Health and disability issues* later in this chapter.

References

The references required are detailed in the Adoption Agencies (Miscellaneous Amendments) Regulations 2013. These include:

- written reports on interviews with three personal referees, not more than one of whom may be a relative;

- written information from the applicants' home local authority;

- a record of any criminal convictions from the police (see below).

In addition, agencies may also make enquiries of some or all of the following: previous partners, adult children, the probation service, the education department, children's schools, the housing department, employers, the bank and/or building society. There is further information about checks and references in Chapter 4. Agency policy and procedure documents should make clear to panel members the range and number of checks and references that the agency requires, as this may be more than the statutory minimum.

Effective Adoption Panels

Criminal background

Regulation 25 of the Adoption Agencies (Miscellaneous Amendments) Regulations 2013 provides that an adoption agency must obtain an enhanced criminal record certificate for the prospective adopter and any member of his/her household aged 18 or over.

An adoption agency may not consider a person suitable to adopt a child if that person or any member of that person's household aged 18 or over –

(a) has been convicted of a specified offence committed at the age of 18 or over; or

(b) has been cautioned by a constable in respect of any such offence which, at the time the caution was given, was admitted.

The Rehabilitation of Offenders Act 1974 does not apply in the case of prospective adopters and therefore all criminal convictions should be listed on the police report. "Specified offences" are listed in Schedule 3 of the Adoption Agencies Regulations 2005. They are in the main offences of violence against children and sexual offences against children.

If between the time of approval and the time of placement of a child, or between placement and the making of an adoption order, a prospective adopter or an adult member of his or her household is convicted of or cautioned for a specified offence, the agency will be required to decide that the prospective adopter is no longer suitable and notify him or her accordingly. Where placement has already occurred, the agency must take immediate steps to remove the child unless the application to adopt has already been issued, in which case it will be a matter for the court. It would be appropriate for the panel to be informed if this occurs.

A criminal record of other offences need not rule out a prospective adopter. However, the nature of the offence, how long ago it was committed, and whether or not it was revealed by the applicant, will all have to be carefully considered. Panel members also need to know the details of any convictions and the applicant's permission for this should be obtained.

It is not appropriate to obtain information about the circumstances of an offence only from the prospective adopter.

Information on a person's police record is obtained from the Disclosure and Barring Service (DBS). From June 2013, the DBS will send the information to the individual concerned. He or she will be required to agree to pass this on to the agency. There is no statutory requirement to update DBS checks at particular intervals – statutory adoption guidance in 2005 suggested a period of every two years but this has not been repeated in the 2013 or draft 2014 guidance.

When prospective adopters are having their annual review, Regulation 30D requires that the review 'should consider the prospective adopter's family circumstances, health, economic circumstances, work commitments, and whether police and medical checks are still up-to-date'. As there is no guidance about how often a DBS check should be updated, this is left to individual agency policy. Prospective adopters can be asked to sign up to the update service (www.gov.uk/dbs-update-service) that allows agencies to check online whether there have been any changes to an adopter's DBS record. There is a small subscription cost to this service paid by the applicant (currently £13 a year) but not to the agency making the check, and as they are carried out online there is no delay in making sure that the DBS check is still current. This would allow the checks to be carried out for the annual review and at the point of matching and application for the adoption order.

Health and disability issues

Medical conditions or disabilities should not necessarily rule out applicants. A health risk assessment should be made by the medical adviser and his or her advice will be extremely important. However, the panel recommendation should involve the views of all panel members.

The following health-related lifestyle factors should also be considered.

- **Smoking.** Does the agency have a policy in relation to applicants who smoke? There is evidence that smoking causes health problems for smokers and that passive smoking can damage the health of others, particularly young children. A Practice Note on smoking (BAAF, 2007) recommends that it is only exceptionally that children under five or those with respiratory problems are placed with carers who smoke.

While stating that 'There is no legal reason why a child cannot be matched with a prospective adopter who smokes', Guidance 4.16 reiterates this: 'A local authority may have to restrict smokers as regards the age and type of child who may be placed with them, especially a child under five or who has a heart or respiratory problem or glue ear.'

- **E-cigarettes.** This is an area of health where research continues. In February 2015, BAAF recommended that there is a low risk to children from the use of e-cigarettes and cautioned that agencies should not use this as a reason to preclude foster carers or adopters purely on this basis but rather that each circumstance should be risk assessed on an individual basis.

  It was noted that the long-term impact of e-cigarettes is unknown, that they appear to have positive benefits for smokers when providing them with a route to abstinence, and that the risk to children from passive smoke is lessened. However, it was noted that 'this needs to be balanced against the risk of providing a model for the child of smoking now, or in the future'.

- **Weight issues.** Obesity can cause health problems as can anorexia or other eating disorders (Mather and Lehner, 2011). Is there evidence of unhealthy eating patterns or limited mobility, either of which could affect their parenting capacity? The medical adviser will advise on this.

- **Drinking.** Excessive alcohol consumption does lead to health problems. For many children in care, alcohol may have been associated with violence and physical abuse. The medical adviser will be able to advise panel members on the Department of Health recommended maximum alcohol consumption amounts.

- **Age.** General health and fitness obviously play an important role in determining an applicant's ability to parent children into adulthood. There is a greater health risk as people age. Agencies have a responsibility to maximise the chances of applicants remaining fit and well into their child's young adulthood. Guidance 3.21 states that: 'Older and more experienced adopters could take on the care of older children provided they will have the health and vigour to meet the child's varied demands in their growing years and to be there for them into adulthood'. Guidance 4.11 cautions that: 'The age of the prospective adopter must also be considered in the light of the age gap between them and the child to be placed with them. Too large a gap may have an adverse effect upon the child and possibly on their relationship with the adoptive parents.' Age is one consideration among many taken into account in assessing the suitability of prospective adopters.

Please also refer to the section on Health and Disability issues in Chapter 4, *Families offering placements*.

Lesbian and gay issues

The Adoption and Children Act 2002 allows unmarried couples, including those of the same sex, to adopt a child jointly.

Gay men and lesbians have been adopting children successfully for a considerable time, either as single adopters or as couples. In the year 2014/15, 800 of the 9,460 adopters approved were gay, lesbian or bisexual. A total of 450 children were adopted by a same-sex couple in the year ending March 2014.

As with all prospective adopters, panel members need to be confident that the stability of their relationship, if they are a couple, has been carefully assessed. Again, in common with all adopters, a strong and diverse support network will be important, with information in the PAR on the input and support from family members and from friends and colleagues that will be available to the adoptive family. Research conducted in the UK (Mellish *et al*, 2013) looked at a sample of heterosexual, lesbian and gay adoptive parents and the outcomes for their children. The clear overall conclusion was that these three types of families were characterised more by similarities than by differences, and the children seemed to have very comparable experiences, regardless of their parents' sexual orientation.

Discipline issues

The Fostering Services Regulations 2002 prohibit the use of corporal punishment by foster carers. Panel members need to be clear whether the agency has a policy on this in relation to adopters. What might the implications be of even a light smack for a child who has previously been physically abused? Does the agency have any policies about the types of discipline that are acceptable or unacceptable? Issues around discipline, including alternatives for managing difficult behaviour, should have been discussed with adopters and incorporated into the prospective adopter's report.

Matching policy in relation to culture, "race", religion and language

The Children Act 1989 requires that:

Before making any decision with respect to a child who they are looking after... a local authority shall give due consideration... to the child's religious persuasion, racial origin and cultural and linguistic background. (Section 22)

However, the amendments made by the 2014 Act to the Adoption and Children Act 2002 have changed the requirement on the adoption agency to 'give due consideration to the child's religious persuasion, racial origin and cultural and religious background'.

The draft Statutory Guidance 2014 sets out the following:

3.4 A prospective adopter can be matched with a child with whom they do not share the same ethnicity, if they can respect, reflect or actively develop a child's racial identity from the point they are matched and as they develop throughout their childhood. The Government is clear that a black, Asian or mixed ethnicity prospective adopter can be a successful adopter of a white or mixed ethnicity child and a white prospective adopter can be a successful adopter of a child who is black, Asian or of mixed ethnicity.

3.5 states that section 1(5) of the Act has been repealed:

To ensure that in placing a child for adoption, differences in ethnicity, religion, culture or language are not given such undue emphasis or prominence that they result in potential placements not being explored or an otherwise unsatisfactory adoption placement not going ahead. This is particularly important when black children wait a year longer to be adopted than white children, and some children simply grow out of the chance of adoption.

3.6 notes that, 'over time, research has established that identifiable differences and lack of a shared heritage do not act as barriers to a successful adoption placement'.

3.7 states that social workers should avoid placing the child's ethnicity above other characteristics without strong, well analysed reasons for doing so and notes that:

An ethnic match is an advantage in an adoption but that is just one of a large number of considerations to be taken account of when matching prospective adopters and children. In practice, ethnicity has frequently been given undue significance in matching.

From a panel's perspective, 3.8 and 3.9 highlight what members should be looking for when considering a match:

What matters in the matching of a child with a prospective adopter of differing ethnicity are the qualities, experiences and attributes the prospective adopter can draw on and their level of understanding of how discrimination and racism operates in society at both an individual and an institutional level. It is therefore vital that the prospective adopter has the openness, strength and insight to support the child or young person if they are confronted by racism when growing up. When such characteristics are present in a prospective adopter the placement can be made with confidence.

The prospective adopter needs to demonstrate that they fully understand that having a child from a different ethnic group will present a number of challenges, not least that there may be visible differences that can affect a child's self-esteem and increase their possible feelings of difference. For example, the child may have to deal with questions from their peers about why they are "different" to their family.

The Guidance gives a similar message in relation to culture, religion and language issues in 3.11–3.13.

Most agencies will have revised their policies in relation to meeting children's cultural and ethnic needs following the change in legislation. This should be included in the pocket on the back cover of this guide.

Permanence

Mention has already been made, earlier in this chapter, of a general childcare policy which the agency may have. This should also be included in the pocket on the back cover. CoramBAAF's position on children's need for permanence is included at the start of the following chapter.

Contact

Adoption with contact is a reality. The fact that a child may need ongoing contact of some sort should not rule out adoption as the plan. This is discussed further in Chapters 3 and 5.

Health and safety issues

Does the agency have any standard requirements with regard to health and safety issues in the applicant's home? If so, a copy of any such document should be attached. It can be helpful for children to have contact with pets. Does the agency have any health, safety and hygiene policies for children placed in relation to any animals, birds, reptiles or insects which applicants may keep in their home? Some agencies use questionnaires to gather information on pets. The practice guide, *Dogs and Pets in Fostering and Adoption* (Adams, 2015) gives useful advice.

Financial matters

Details of the agency's policy and procedures in relation to financial support should be included in the pocket on the back cover. Panel members should have information on the agency's practice and procedures in relation to financial support for adopters, child arrangements order allowances, special guardianship allowances, maintenance payments between placement for adoption and the adoption order, and settling-in grants and payments for equipment or house extensions. Panel members may wish to discuss these with the agency.

Family work patterns

Does the agency have a policy in relation to applicants working outside the home? It is probably most helpful to be fairly flexible about this while recognising, at the matching stage, that some children will need a parent at home with them full time for a considerable period. The support that the agency is able to offer, including the provision of financial support, may be crucial.

One adoptive parent (in a couple) is eligible for statutory adoption leave from work for a year. The first 39 weeks is paid, the subsequent period is unpaid. The other parent is eligible for two weeks "paternity" leave. Couples can choose who takes which leave, e.g. a male partner could take the adoption leave and a female partner the "paternity" leave. The Children and Families Act 2014 introduced shared parental leave for adopters and brought adoption pay and leave into line with maternity benefits. It also introduced an entitlement to Statutory Adoption Pay and Leave for prospective adopters who were offering a concurrent placement or an FFA placement from the point of placement.

Adoption support services

The package of adoption support services may well be a crucial factor when panel members are considering the viability of a placement. Panel members in local authorities need to be clear about what and how ongoing support is offered by the local authority, including help to access specialist health and education services when necessary. Panel members in voluntary adoption agencies also need to know about the adoption support services offered by their agency.

The placing local authority will be responsible for assessing adoption support needs for three years after the adoption order, after which this reverts to the area authority. Regular financial support and support in relation to contact remain the placing authority's responsibility.

A copy of the Adoption Passport, written to inform prospective adopters about support and how to access it, is available at www.first4adoption.org.uk/adoption-support/the-adoption-passport/.

Placements with family members or existing foster carers

All the above issues need equally careful consideration when birth family members or existing foster carers are being considered as permanent parents for a child. Guidance 4.13 recognises that local authorities are required to consider a placement with relatives if the child is unable to return to birth parents and that fostering or special guardianship may be the right plan, but states 'the appropriateness of adoption by a relative should not be automatically ruled out'. Guidance 4.14 states that there may be some circumstances where the security provided by the irrevocability of an adoption order and its lifelong effect would be best for the child and outweigh the potential drawbacks of the "skewing" of relationships. It references case law to the effect that 'there is no presumption that a special guardianship order will be preferable to an adoption order if the placement is with a relative'. The benefits for the child of remaining within their birth family and/or of retaining an existing strong attachment need to be taken into account. However, these placements should not be viewed as a fait accompli. Research by Biehal *et al* (2010) found that adoption by their foster carer had positive outcomes for children, and Dibben and Howorth (2016) have argued that this is an underused resource for children needing adoption. Statutory Adoption Guidance 3.79 states that:

Foster carers who express an interest in adopting children in their care should be given advice about the fact that the adoption procedures apply in their case as in any other...Although foster carers have a legal right to institute their own adoption application, once the child has lived with them for a specific period of time, the local authority should encourage them to participate in the adoption agency process.

Local authorities should use a fast-track approval process for foster carers adopting, where they enter the process at Stage Two – see Chapter 4.

Members of staff

Good practice suggests that applicants who are members of staff working for the adoption agency or for the Children and Families part of the Children's Services Department should apply to adopt to another agency. Consideration should be given to whether this requirement should also apply to all staff working for the Children's Services Department, in the interests of confidentiality and fairness. In the rare cases where the member of staff is interested in adopting a specific child or children looked after by their employing agency, the consideration of the matching could also be undertaken by another agency's panel.

Duration of approval

Regulations require an adoption agency to review, whenever it considers it necessary, and at least annually, the approval of prospective adopters who do not have a child placed or are not, in the case of an intercountry adopter, committed to proceeding with the adoption of a specific child. The agency is only required to refer the case to the panel if it considers the adopters are no longer suitable to adopt a child. In this situation, the same procedure must be followed as for the consideration of new prospective adopters (AA(MA)R 2013, 30D).

Previous guidance specified that police checks should be renewed every two years. Provided that prospective adopters have subscribed to the DBS online update service, their DBS police check can be updated online at any time. There is no statutory requirement about updating other checks and references but it would be good practice to do this every two years. CoramBAAF recommends that a medical update is obtained every two years. The agency should have clear written procedures on this.

The agency also needs to be clear about, and to make clear to the panel and to prospective adopters, what the procedure will be when a family has a disrupted placement before an adoption order is made. Statutory Guidance sets out that a disruption of a placement would be a reason to hold an early review where the family wishes to continue as approved adopters.

Representations and complaints

The Children Act 1989 complaints procedure, which is set out in The Children Act Representations Procedure (England) Regulations 2006, requires local authorities to establish a procedure for considering representations, including complaints. These must be in relation to a specific child. They could include representations about cases that the panel had considered. For example, a foster carer might complain that, although adoption was the agency plan for a child in her care, she was still waiting two years later and nothing seemed to be happening. Agencies should normally inform panel members of representations about cases that the panel has considered.

Adoptive applicants can make representations, including complaints, to a local authority if the local authority has a power or duty to provide them with a service. Local authorities do have a general duty under section 2 of the Adoption and Children Act 2002 to provide services for people wishing to adopt a child. Representations would have to be in relation to the service offered (or not offered) and would not be a method of appealing against an agency decision about suitability to adopt.

Representations and complaints can only be made to voluntary adoption agencies in relation to children for whom they are providing a service who are not looked after by a local authority. Adoptive applicants have the right to make representations to voluntary agencies under the Voluntary Adoption Agencies and the Adoption Agencies (Miscellaneous Amendments) Regulations 2003, Regulation 11. National Minimum Standards require that voluntary agencies should have procedures to enable users of their services to make representations, including complaints, about any aspect of the adoption service provided. It would be helpful to include a copy of these procedures in the pocket on the back cover.

When an agency decision-maker is proposing not to approve prospective adopters as suitable to adopt, they are entitled to an independent review of their case. This process is described in more detail in Chapter 4 in the section about the Independent Review Mechanism (IRM).

References

Adams P (2015) *Dogs and Pets in Fostering and Adoption*, London: BAAF

BAAF (2007) *Reducing the Risks of Environmental Tobacco Smoke for Looked After Children and their Carers*, Practice Note 51, London: BAAF

Biehal N, Ellison S, Baker C and Sinclair I (2010) *Belonging and Permanence: Outcomes in long-term foster care and adoption*, London: BAAF

Coram Centre for Early Permanence (2013) *Fostering for Adoption Practice Guidance*, London: Coram

Department for Education (2012) *Children Looked After in England 2011*, London: Department for Education

Department for Education and Skills (2005) *Children Looked After in England (including adoptions and care leavers): 2003–2004*, Norwich: The Stationery Office

Dibben E and Howorth V (2016) *Adoption by Foster Carers: A guide to preparing, assessing and supporting foster carers adopting children in their care*, London: CoramBAAF

Jenny C, Roesler TA and Poyer KL (1994) 'Are children at risk for sexual abuse by homosexuals?', *Pediatrics*, 94(1), pp 41–4

Mellish L, Jennings S, Tasker F, Lamb M and Golombok S (2013) *Gay, Lesbian and Heterosexual Adoptive Families: Family relationships, child adjustment and adopters' experiences*, London: BAAF

Sellick C, Thoburn J and Philpot T (2004) *What Works in Adoption and Foster Care?*, London: Barnardo's

3 Considering adoption for a child

Introduction

Children normally experience permanence from the life-long commitment of their family network, which provides for them an experience of belonging, continuity and ongoing support.

Permanence is essential for children in order to provide them with a foundation from which to develop their identity, values and relationships throughout their childhood and into adulthood.

For most children permanence is achieved within their family of origin and every effort should, therefore, be made to sustain this situation. When separation cannot be avoided, the child should be restored to their birth parents or family as quickly as possible.

Where this is not in the child's best interests, an alternative family should be found that can provide continuous care and commitment to the child into adulthood. Such a family should be well equipped to meet the child's needs and should, if possible, reflect the child's ethnic, religious and cultural heritage, acknowledge and respect their family of origin and, where appropriate, maintain ongoing links and relationships that are responsive to changing needs.

This search needs to be balanced against the importance of minimising any delay in placing the child.

The routes to permanence are varied depending on the needs of the individual child. For some separated children, adoption will provide the best means of ensuring legal security together with lifelong commitments; for others, permanence might best be achieved through special guardianship, child arrangements orders or foster care.

Whichever route to permanence is most appropriate, help and support to child and family, before and after placement, are essential.

Adoption plans for children – the involvement of a court

It is fairly rare for birth parents to voluntarily relinquish their child for adoption. In most cases where the local authority decides that adoption is the best plan for a child, it will need to apply to a court for a care order and a placement order. The placement order will authorise it to place the child for adoption.

Planning for permanence for the child will start from when the child is taken into care, or even before this. It will be considered at the first review, after the child has been in care for a month, and Guidance 2.4 specifies that an appropriate permanence plan should be identified *no later than* at the second statutory review – the four month review.

There will have been ongoing work and discussion with birth parents and with the child and other family members, as appropriate, and information on their wishes and feelings will have been gathered. When a review decides that adoption is the preferred option for permanence, there must be additional counselling and additional information will be gathered to complete a Child's Permanence Report (CPR). This report, expert reports prepared in connection with the court proceedings, or a summary of these and the views of the children's guardian, will then be submitted to the senior manager in the local authority who is a designated decision-maker for adoption. If he or she confirms the adoption plan, an application will be made to court for a care order and placement order. The court will have the responsibility of scrutinising the plan and birth parents will have the opportunity to contest the plan.

Adoption panels used to consider all adoption plans for children. However, the Adoption Agencies (Panel and Consequential Amendments) Regulations amended the Adoption Agencies Regulations 2005 with effect from 1 September 2012. The amended Regulation 17 states that a local authority adoption agency 'may not refer the case to the adoption panel' if there will be court involvement and scrutiny because an application for a placement order will be required were the agency decision-maker to decide that the child should be placed for adoption. This will be where the birth parents do not consent to adoption, where care proceedings are ongoing or where the child has no parents. These cases must be submitted directly to the decision-maker for a decision.

There is no provision for referring a case to panel for advice. The guidance is clear that in cases where the court will be involved, referral to panel for any reason is prohibited and would be a breach both of the regulations and of Data Protection principles. However, the decision-maker may discuss the case with the agency adviser, medical issues with the medical adviser and seek legal advice (Guidance 1.55).

The panel's role in adoption plans for children

The adoption panel must continue to be involved in cases where there is no court scrutiny of the adoption plan because birth parents are in agreement with it. Guidance 2.64 clarifies that these will be cases where a child is voluntarily accommodated or relinquished for adoption and birth parents consent to adoption or where there is already a care order and the parents indicate that they will consent to adoption.

In cases where there is already a care order and the parents indicate that they will consent to adoption, but the agency considers that there is a possibility that they will change their minds, it may either present the case to panel or directly to the decision-maker, as an application for a placement order may be necessary. The agency must take into account the effect on the child of any unnecessary delay.

If such a case is presented to panel, it must consider carefully the legal advice given. The panel is required to consider whether an application should be made for a placement order and it may, although probably very rarely, give such advice to the agency. The issues to be balanced are the security given by a placement order but the delay in the placement process which an application to court will cause.

The panel will mainly be considering adoption plans for babies and young children relinquished by their parents for adoption. However, there could be some older children, possibly already on care orders, whose parents are now agreeing to adoption and for whom a placement order is not thought necessary. The rest of the chapter includes information that will be relevant to older children but may be less so or not at all in relation to relinquished infants.

Relinquishment for adoption of an infant aged less than six weeks

When a pregnant woman approaches an adoption agency wishing to place her baby for adoption, she should be counselled about the options for the child's future care and about the adoption process. The expected child's father should also be counselled, if possible, as described later. If adoption is considered to be the best plan for the child, a CPR and a health report should be started and it should be arranged for the agency medical adviser and panel to be ready to consider the case as soon as possible after the baby is born. Family finding should also start. When the baby is born the child's birth parents should again be counselled. If they still want their child to be adopted, the CPR and health report should be completed and, if possible, adopters identified. Guidance 2.47 states that 'with enough preparation the adoption panel should be ready to consider the case within a day or so of the birth'. Formal consent to the child's adoption is not legally possible until the child is six weeks old. However, written agreement to the adoption plan can be obtained earlier and, as described in 'what next?', the child can be matched with prospective adopters at the same panel as considers the plan.

Panel functions

The adoption panel must consider:

...the case of every child referred to it by the adoption agency and make a recommendation to the agency as to whether the child should be placed for adoption. (AAR 18(1))

It must also consider and may give advice to the agency about:

(a) the arrangements which the agency proposes to make for allowing any person contact with the child; and

(b) where the agency is a local authority, whether an application should be made by the authority for a placement order in respect of the child. (AAR 18(3))

Timescales

Guidance 2.2 specifies that:

- *The child's need for a permanent home should be addressed and a permanence plan made at the **four month** review.*

- *The adoption panel should receive all necessary information from the agency within **six weeks** of the completion of the child's permanence report.*

- *The adoption panel's recommendation on whether the child should be placed for adoption should be made within **two months** of a review* *where adoption has been identified as the permanence plan.*

NMS 17.11 states that 'The decision-maker makes a considered decision that takes account of all the information available to them, including the recommendation of the adoption panel and, where applicable, the independent review panel, within **seven working days** of receipt of the recommendation and final set of panel minutes'.

The four-month review is the second review held four months after a child starts to be looked after by a local authority. However, the plan may not be adoption at this stage. It could be a plan for the child's permanent placement back at home with parent(s) or with extended family members.

Guidance is clear that, although these timescales should generally be adhered to, the paramount consideration must always be the welfare of the child. Where the agency is unable to comply with a timescale or decides not to, the reasons for this should be recorded on the child's case record.

Panel members should also ask the reasons for what may appear to be delay in getting a case to panel. While thorough work must be done with birth parents and extended family (see later section), this must be done within a timescale that meets the child's needs to be settled in their permanent family as soon as possible.

Information required

Regulations require that the panel is sent the child's permanence report (CPR).

The medical adviser is required to prepare a summary of 'the state of the child's health, his health history and any need for health care which may arise in the future' (AAR 17(b)) for inclusion in the child's permanence report. It will probably be helpful if the medical adviser can also summarise relevant health information about the child's parents and siblings. The medical adviser will have the full health reports available at panel but these will not be circulated to each panel member unless so advised by the medical adviser. The panel may, however, request further information, which could include some or all of the detailed medical reports.

Other specialist reports may be helpful if they contribute to a comprehensive picture of the child's needs.

The panel must consider all the reports presented to it and 'may request the agency to obtain any other relevant information which the panel considers necessary' (AAR 18).

The agency is required to meet such requests as far as it can.

If the panel decides to defer consideration of a case until it has fuller or more adequate information, a date should always be set, probably the next panel meeting, for the re-presentation of the case. The agency adviser to the panel has primary responsibility for "gatekeeping" and for ensuring the adequacy of the information sent to panel members.

Any concerns about the quality of information should be raised at the panel meeting and minuted. Either the Chair or the agency adviser should take the matter up with the child's social worker and his or her manager, or with senior managers.

Legal advice

The panel must obtain legal advice. This can be given verbally or in writing. It would be good practice for the legal adviser to be present at panel if possible to answer any questions.

People attending the panel

The child's social worker will attend and it is important for his or her manager to attend too if at all possible. It can be very helpful if the child's current carer also attends. It is not usual for either the child or his or her birth parents to attend, although some agencies have offered this opportunity and have found that it can be helpful. It is important that panel members are fully informed about the views of the child and his or her birth parents. They could be invited to write or send a recording to panel members or to the Chair, if they wish.

Welfare of children

The panel, like the agency, is bound by the duty set out in Section 1 of the Adoption and Children Act 2002. This is given in full in Chapter 2 and should be the overarching context in which the plan for a child is considered. Key points are that:

- the paramount concern should be the welfare of the child, throughout his or her life;
- the child should be involved and consulted at all stages in the adoption process and his or her wishes and feelings taken into account in a way which is sensitive to, and consistent with, his or her age and understanding.

The child's permanence report

The information to be included in this report is detailed in Schedule 1, parts 1 and 3, of the AAR, and in AAR 17. It must include the following.

Information about the child (Schedule 1 Part 1)

- Factual information about the child, e.g. date of birth, ethnicity, religion, legal status.
- Chronology of the child's care since birth.
- Description of personality and of social, emotional and behavioural development.
- Education issues including any special needs.
- Relationships with birth parents, siblings and others, including:
  - the likelihood of the relationship continuing and the value to the child of it doing so, and
  - the ability and willingness of parents or others to meet the child's needs.
- Current contact arrangements with parents, relatives and others.
- Interests, likes and dislikes.

Information on the child's family and others (Schedule 1 part 3)

- Current factual information on the child's parents, siblings and other relatives.
- A family tree, including information about grandparents, aunts and uncles and parents.
- Clarification of who the father is and whether he has parental responsibility.
- Chronology of each parent since birth, including educational and employment history.
- Parents' experience of being parented.
- Their relationship, past and present.
- Details of wider family, their role and importance.
- Their parenting capacity, particularly their ability and willingness to parent the child.

Additional information (AAR 17)

- A health summary by the medical adviser on the child's health, health history and anticipated future health needs.
- The child's wishes and feelings about:
  - adoption
  - religious and cultural upbringing
  - contact with birth family and others
- Wishes and feelings of parents about:
  - the child
  - the plan, including religious and cultural upbringing
  - future contact
- Agency's views on and plans for contact.
- Assessment of the child's emotional and behavioural development.
- Assessment of parenting capacity of parents.
- Chronology of decision and actions taken by the agency.
- An analysis of options for future care and 'why placement for adoption is considered the preferred option' (AAR 17(1)).

CoramBAAF has published the Form CPR/Annex B report, a template that enables agencies to be compliant with the regulations in relation to the child's permanence report and to use the same report for the Annex B report for the placement order. It is up to agencies to decide which format to use.

Issues to consider

The following list indicates some of the issues that panel members will need to consider when reading reports on children and formulating questions for the child's workers and carers. It is not intended to be exhaustive and other issues may well need to be addressed in individual cases.

The child's birth family

Panel members will need to be clear about how and why the child came to the attention of children's services and why the plan is now adoption. They will need to know what work has been done with birth family members and whether anything more could be done to help the child's birth family provide a home for him or her. The agency has a duty to counsel birth parents in relation to the adoption plan. NMS 12.3 requires them to have access to a support worker independent of the child's social worker from the time adoption is identified as the plan for the child. Panel members must be clear that all other possible options for the child to remain with his or her birth parents or extended family or other people significant to the child have been fully explored. They need to be clear what the views of the child's birth parents and other family members are about the adoption plan.

Birth fathers without parental responsibility

In particular, panel members should check that the child's father, whether or not he is married to the mother, has been contacted and his wishes and feelings ascertained. This should be done unless there are clear reasons against it. There is useful guidance and case law on this in Guidance 2.34 – 2.42. The paramount consideration, as always, is the welfare of the child. Guidance 2.39 states that 'where the agency considers that it is appropriate – i.e. that it is in the child's best interests – the agency must take all reasonable steps to trace and counsel the child's unmarried father, if his identity is known'. The local authority has 'discretion to do this against the wishes of the mother'. However, it is acknowledged that case law *Re: C* confirmed that 'it was not automatically "appropriate" for the agency to make contact with the father solely in order to obtain background information.' The birth mother's wishes are a factor and, crucially, in the case of a father without parental responsibility, the role he has played in the child's life and in life with the mother and any other siblings. Each situation must be considered carefully on its own merits and is a matter for the agency's or court's discretion. This would be an area where the panel will want to seek and receive written legal advice.

Extended family members

Guidance 2.33 acknowledges that 'where the parents wish to conceal from members of their family the fact of the child's existence, or the fact that they are seeking adoption, the agency will be faced with a conflict between the parents' right to privacy and the child's right to know, and perhaps the chance of being brought up by their extended family. Where the agency considers it is likely to be in the child's interests to be given this opportunity, it should encourage the parents to consider the matter from the point of view of the child. '... Agencies should avoid giving parents any undertakings that the birth or the adoption will be kept secret. Each case will have to be considered on its own facts.'

Panel members should check whether birth parents have seen the permanence report. Guidance 2.60 states that birth family members should be asked to check the accuracy of factual information. In addition, the birth parents 'should be shown those parts of the report which set out their views and wishes, and given the opportunity, if they so wish, to express these in their own words'. The Guidance continues: 'Where the child is old enough, they should also be encouraged to confirm that their views have been accurately stated'. The CPR should make it clear whether the parents have seen the CPR or parts of it, and include any comments they have expressed on it.

(See also sections on contact issues below.)

What does the child understand and feel about what has happened and what is planned?

The child's wishes and feelings must be ascertained and given due consideration having regard to his or her age and understanding when making any decision about adoption for him or her (section 1 of the Adoption and Children Act 2002 quoted in full in Chapter 2).

The child will have experienced separations and loss and may well be confused, angry, sad and bewildered. It will be important for panel members to try and assess the child's understanding of what has happened and why, and of what is planned for them. Who is doing direct work with the child and how is this progressing? It can be very helpful for the panel to hear first hand from the child's foster carer or residential social worker, as well as from their social worker. Is there further work that needs to be done before the child can be placed in a new family?

Identity issues

Is there clear written information on the child's cultural, racial, religious and linguistic heritage? It will be important for panel members to have as much information as possible about the child's birth father as well as their mother. What sense does the child have of his or her heritage and identity? Is the child living with carers who reflect the child's identity? Panel members should consider whether there is any work that relates to identity and which needs to be done before the child can be placed in a new family and should find out what the plan for this is.

Attachment issues

The child's early attachment experience will be a crucial factor in his or her ability to grow into a secure, self-confident person able to make new attachments. Poor early experience of attachments that may have been inconsistent, abusive, neglectful or constantly changing will have a profound effect on the child and will have considerable long-term implications for him or her and for the new parents. Panel members should ensure that they have full information on the child's attachment experience from birth. It will be important to have information about the quality of the child's attachment to the current carers and other significant people. Panel members should ascertain what help and support will be given to the child, to the carers and to the new family in the process of building, maintaining and transferring attachments.

Abuse and neglect issues

Some of the children whose cases come before the panel may have experienced abuse, either physical or sexual or both, and neglect, either physical or emotional, or all of these. It will be important for panel members to be clear about the known facts about what has happened to the child. They also need to be aware that much more may have happened than is currently known. It is important to consider the following: What impact do the child's experiences of abuse and neglect have on their functioning and behaviour? What help is being given to the child and their current carers to deal with these issues? What are the long-term implications for a new family and what future help and support are the child and their new parents going to need?

Behavioural issues

Panel members will need up-to-date information on the child's behaviour in different settings, for example, in the foster home and at school. How does the child relate to other children and to adults? Information on how the child reacts to change will be important. Panel members should bear in mind that foster carers are used to looking after children with challenging behaviour who then move on and that children sometimes "contain" their feelings and behaviour until they are somewhere secure. There is thus a possibility that the child's problems may be underestimated. What help are the child and the carers currently receiving to manage any challenging behaviour and what is likely to be needed in the future?

Health and disability issues

Children for whom adoption is the plan are required by AAR 15 to have a comprehensive medical assessment and examination covering physical, developmental and emotional issues. The medical adviser may advise that this is not necessary if, for instance, there is already a report which includes the required information (Guidance 2.49 and 2.50). It is helpful if the medical adviser is also the doctor involved in the health assessment of children who are to be placed for adoption. This may not be possible but when it is, the medical adviser will usually be the only panel member who has met the child.

As well as evaluating the child's physical and emotional health and development, the medical adviser will also gather as much information as possible about the health of his or her birth parents and siblings and about any genetic implications for the child. He or she will also arrange for any further tests or examinations or treatment which may be necessary for the child. A summary by the medical adviser of the health history and state of health of the child and his or her parents, with comments on the implications for adoption and on how any special health needs of the child might be met, will be included in the child's permanence report, while the medical adviser retains the fuller reports. It is important that the medical adviser is available to interpret and advise on any health issues. If the child has a need arising from a particular health problem, condition or disability which affects day-to-day living, it will be important for panel members to have information from the current carers about this.

Education issues

Panel members will need written information on the child's current functioning and likely future needs. This should be covered in the child's permanence report supplemented as necessary by a school report, an educational psychologist's report, and the current carer's observations.

Needs of siblings

The panel should consider each child as an individual in his or her own right, with needs as described above, as well as a member of a sibling group.

Panel members should also raise the following issues:

- Who are the child's siblings?

- Why are siblings being placed separately if this is the proposed plan?

- Why are siblings, who may have very great and perhaps conflicting needs, being placed together if this is the proposed plan? It will be important to check whether siblings have been involved together in abusive situations and, if they have, whether they can break the abusive ways of relating that they have learned, as long as they remain together. Has appropriate work been undertaken with these children to facilitate change?

- How do the children get on with each other? The observations of their carers will be important and the agency may also have completed the sibling relationship checklist in *Together or Apart? Assessing brothers and sisters for permanent placement* (Lord and Borthwick, 2008).

- What are the wishes and feelings of the children themselves about being placed together or separately?

- If the children are currently living apart but the plan is for placement together, what is being done to maintain or build a relationship between them?

- If the plan is for separate placements for siblings, what sort of contact between them is planned?

- What additional financial support may be available for a new family taking on a sibling group? Large sibling groups of five or six children can be found adoptive families but a package of financial support is often a vital factor in the viability of these placements.

Regular financial support can be paid to enable a sibling group to be placed together and to enable a child to join his or her siblings in an adoptive family (ASR 8(2)(c)).

Following a consultation on the placement of siblings, the 2014 Act introduced an amendment to the Adoption Agencies Regulations in relation to the placement of siblings. This is covered as follows in the Draft Statutory Guidance (2014).

3.15 There should be a clear decision making process which enables social workers to decide early whether it is in the best interests of each child to be placed together or separately, and the impact on each child of that decision. The decision making process should be set out clearly with the supporting information and evidence so that all the professionals who are involved in making decisions about each child's future can see how and why the decision was reached. It will also be important in future for the child, as an adult, to be able to see how and why a decision was reached. The decision should be based on a balanced assessment of the individual needs of each child in the group, and the likely or possible consequences of each option on each child. Agencies may wish to have a formal assessment process in place to assist with the analysis and decision making.

SG 3.16 notes that:

There are many factors that may need to be considered in reaching a decision on whether to place siblings together or separately. These will include:

- *the nature of the sibling group – for example, do the siblings know each other, how are they related;*

- *whether the children have formed an attachment, and if so the nature of that attachment (secure, insecure or otherwise);*

- *the health needs of each child;*

- *each child's view (noting that a child's views and perceptions will change over time);*

- *other relevant factors.*

This means that the agency is better able to make robust, evidenced decisions on whether it is in the interests of each child to be placed separately or together.

Permanence options

The child's permanence report must contain an analysis of the options for the future care of the child which have been considered by the agency and why placement for adoption is considered the preferred option AAR 17(1)(i).

- **Adoption** offers legal security to a child, giving their adoptive parent exclusive and irrevocable parental responsibility. The legal parent–child relationship is for life. However, some form of contact with the child's birth family is quite common. This may be an annual exchange of letters via the adoption agency or it may be face-to-face contact, possibly with siblings or grandparents or sometimes with birth parents. Adoptive families have the right to be assessed for a range of support services at any time until the child is 18, and a range of services, including financial support, is often in place from the time of the child's placement.

Other permanence options are:

- **Returning the child** to his or her parent(s) with support where necessary. This is the preferred option if it can offer good enough and safe care to the child. The reasons why this is not possible must be clearly given and evidenced in the permanence report.

- **Placement with a relative.** This should have been explored, preferably using a Family Group Conference to mobilise all family members and to involve them in plans for the child's future. Relatives on both the mother's and the father's side of the family should be described in the report as well as their views and capacity to care for the child. A placement with relatives could be secured via adoption, special guardianship, a child arrangements order, long-term fostering or possibly with no order.

- **Remaining with existing foster carers.** This will provide continuity for the child and may well be what a child wants. Permanence could be achieved via adoption, special guardianship, long-term fostering or a child arrangements order. Guidance 3.79 states that foster carers who express an interest in adopting children in their care should be given advice about the procedures that will apply in their case. The benefits of continuity and of maintaining a good attachment and avoiding a move for a child have been highlighted in research. The benefits should always be weighed against other factors which may be seen as less positive. The 2014 Act has made it clear that a transracial placement is not a reason not to pursue a placement in itself and where there are identified security issues relating to the carers being known to the parents, Dibben and Howorth (2016) have highlighted the importance of discussing with foster carers how these risks may be addressed and give examples of carers who had moved home or area to minimise these risks. Where the carers are offering long-term fostering when the child needs legal permanence, the local authority will need to consider whether it is worth making compromises for the benefits offered by the placement.

- **Long-term fostering.** Research indicates that this can provide a sense of permanence for some children and young people. Their birth parents retain parental responsibility and may remain in quite frequent contact. Foster carers can work in partnership with the local authority and receive a fostering allowance that is not means tested and may include a fee. The child will receive ring-fenced services available to looked after children, including leaving care provision. However, he or she will remain a "foster child", subject to statutory visits and reviews, which may be felt to be stigmatising by some children. The foster carers will not have parental responsibility, which is shared instead by the local authority and birth parents. The local authority could decide to move the child and the parents could decide to apply to court for revocation of a care order. So, legally the placement is not secure, although in practice, with co-operation between all the parties, it may feel so to the child.

- **Child arrangements order.** Foster carers or relatives could apply to court and be granted a child arrangements order. This can last until the child is 18, gives the carer parental responsibility but does not remove this from the birth parent(s). The child ceases to be looked after by the local authority, although the authority has discretion to pay a child arrangements order allowance to the carers. Support can be offered by the local authority although there is no statutory requirement to do so, other than to the child as " a child in need".

- **Special guardianship.** This is an order introduced under the Adoption and Children Act 2002. Guidance on special guardianship describes the need for 'an alternative legal status for children that offered greater security than long-term fostering but without the absolute legal severance that stems from an adoption order'. This was based on research indicating that 'children generally preferred the sense of security that adoption gives them over long-term foster placements. However, research indicated that there was a significant group of children, mainly older, who did not wish to make an absolute legal break with their birth family that is associated with adoption.'

Special guardianship does not remove parental responsibility from birth parents but it enables the special guardian to exercise their parental responsibility to the exclusion of all others, other than in a few very specific situations. The child is no longer looked after. However, if they were previously looked after, they and their special guardian(s) must, if they request, be assessed for support services, including financial support. These services equate almost exactly with adoption support services, but also include access for the formerly looked after child to leaving care provisions. Special guardianship orders are made by a court and can be made in favour of one or more people, who do not need to be married. Orders can be revoked, but the thresholds for applying are high, and so they offer legal security, even if it falls short of that offered by adoption.

- **Residential care** is a possible option for a child with very significant disabilities or other special needs for whom no family can be found, or for whom family care is not feasible or appropriate. This may only become the plan when the agency has failed to find a family for the child or when several family placements have disrupted. For a small group of children and young people, it may offer the best form of care and the one most acceptable to them.

Practice considerations in relation to permanence options

Guidance on adoption and permanence panels in 1.23–1.25 acknowledges that fostering plans for children are not required by regulations to be considered by a panel. It goes on to say:

However, given the significance of long-term fostering many agencies have established adoption and permanence panels, which combine knowledge and experience of adoption and fostering and enable these two permanence options to be considered by one panel.

Although it may be clear that a child needs permanence in a new family, the options for achieving this need careful scrutiny and for some children it may be very difficult to find a new permanent family. An adoption and permanence panel would be well placed to consider adoption or long-term foster care. It may recommend that the child should be placed for adoption, or, if it considers that adoption would not best meet the child's needs, it could advise that the child should be placed into long-term foster care. This reduces the time needed to identify the type of placement that is most likely to meet the child's needs by avoiding consideration of adoption or fostering at separate panel meetings.

Some children will be referred to an adoption and permanence panel for whom the plan is adoption and others will be referred for whom the plan is long-term fostering or possibly special guardianship or a child arrangements order. In each case, panel members should keep in mind the strengths and limitations of all the permanence options described in the preceding section.

Clearly a consideration of the child returning to one or both birth parents must come first. This should be followed by a consideration of extended family members. This option and that of remaining with existing foster carers could be via adoption, special guardianship, a child arrangements order or long-term fostering.

All these permanence options need to be kept in mind before a permanence recommendation is made. The advantage of an adoption and permanence panel is that it is not limited to only making adoption recommendations. Even if an adoption recommendation is made, that panel can acknowledge that, for some children, it may be extremely difficult to find an adoptive family. Case law *Re: P* 2008 clarifies that dual planning for adoption and long-term fostering is possible with a concurrent search for adoptive and fostering placements. The panel will need detailed information on adoption family finding to ensure that enough efforts have been made to achieve an adoptive placement.

Contact issues

The panel must consider and may give advice about the 'arrangements which the agency proposes to make for allowing any person contact with the child'

(AAR 18(3)). The "welfare checklist" in section 1 of the Adoption and Children Act 2002 (see Chapter 2), which must be considered in relation to every case, includes a duty to consider the child's relationship with relatives and others. The agency's views on contact and plans for this must be included in the child's permanence report and this must include both the child's wishes and feelings and those of his or her parents and other relatives.

Panel members need to understand and to check that birth parents understand that, once a local authority is authorised to place a child for adoption, either because it has a placement order or because parents have given formal consent, there is no presumption for or against contact. Any previous contact order ceases to have effect as does the 1989 Children Act duty to promote contact. The individual child's welfare becomes the paramount consideration in any consideration of contact arrangements.

Any previous contact order ceases to have effect, as does the 1989 Children Act duty to promote contact. The individual child's welfare becomes the paramount consideration in any consideration of contact arrangements.

The 2014 Act introduced new Regulations that enable the courts to consider making contact orders at the adoption order stage.

Statutory Guidance (2014) sets out that the court can make an order under section 51A of the Act that either provides for contact or prohibits contact between the child and their birth family members. It is recognised that these orders:

are likely to be relatively rare at the adoption order stage, and where some form of continuing contact is proposed, whether direct or indirect, it is more likely that this will be a matter for agreement between the person concerned and the adopters. The court may however make a note on the court file about the agreement reached.

Similarly, an application can be made post-adoption at any time for an order to set up or prohibit contact.

The adopters or the child may apply for such an order without the leave of the court, while any other person, including the child's birth parents and other birth relatives, e.g. grandparents or siblings, would need the court's leave to apply for such an order.

The Guidance suggests the need for such orders will be rare and they are most likely to be used to prohibit contact where there has been unwanted contact between a birth parent and the child through, for example, social media, but equally Regulation 51 could be used to challenge a situation where adopters have not maintained contact with a child's sibling.

A plan for face-to-face contact with parents, birth relatives and other people significant to the child need not rule out adoption. However, it will be important to be clear about the purpose of future contact and the value to the child. Panel members should ask about the type, frequency and quality of current contact and who is involved.

- What are the plans for contact after placement?
- Do the birth family members agree with the contact plans?
- What are the child's wishes and feelings about contact after adoption?
- What help and support do the agency plan to offer to facilitate contact arrangements after adoption?

Giving advice on whether a placement order should be applied for

The panel must consider this and may give advice to the agency.

In cases where parents do not agree with the adoption plan, the local authority has no choice but to apply for a placement order and the case will not come to panel.

If there is already a care order in place and the parents consent to adoption, the local authority may either apply for a placement order or it may place for adoption with consent. This consent must be witnessed by a CAFCASS officer. Placing with consent will avoid the work and possible delay of a court hearing. However, there is the risk that the parents could change their minds. Should they do this before the child is placed, the placement would need to be delayed until a court had made a placement order. Should they do this after placement but before an application for an adoption order, the local authority could apply for a placement order, which would prevent the child's removal. A possible advantage of applying for a placement order before placement is that it would give relatives the chance to be heard and to give their views on the adoption plan.

A placement order may be revoked on the application of the local authority or the child. Anyone else may only apply with the leave of the court and only if the child has not yet been placed for adoption. Unless revoked, a placement order will continue in force until the child is adopted, reaches 18, marries or forms a civil partnership.

Conditional or "in principle" recommendations

Although the Guidance makes no explicit reference to not making "in principle" recommendations, it makes clear that the decision-maker's decision must be based on a definite recommendation.

The agency must have a clear care plan for adoption before it refers the case to the panel for recommendation that the child should be placed for adoption. This cannot be conditional on the outcome of any assessments of birth parents or extended family members, or for any other reason.

What next?

A panel recommends whether a child should be placed for adoption and the agency then makes a decision about this. The panel may then not hear about the child again until a matching with prospective adopters is presented.

Guidance 4.33 clarifies that, in appropriate cases, to avoid unnecessary delay, recommendations about placement can be made at the same panel meeting as recommendations about the plan for the child and/or the approval of adopters. It states that 'this will be appropriate in a case where a baby is being relinquished for adoption…In this case the recommendation that the child should be placed for adoption can be made at the same time as the recommendation that they should be placed with a particular prospective adopter. Similarly, where a child is living with foster carers who wish to adopt them, it may be appropriate for the recommendation as to their suitability to be made at the same panel as the recommendation about the placement of the child with them, or even, occasionally, for all three recommendations to be made at the same meeting.'

Panel members could ask at the meeting at which they make their recommendation about what actual steps will be taken to identify a family. The Adoption Agencies (Miscellaneous Amendments) Regulations 2013 require that, unless the agency is considering specific prospective adopters for the child, he or she must be referred to the Adoption Register as soon as possible, and no later than three months after the adoption decision.

The panel should also request regular, perhaps three- or six-monthly reports on waiting children and on waiting families. Guidance 1.34 specifies that 'the agency adviser should also update the panel on the general progress of cases it has considered. This is particularly important where the panel's recommendation or advice was not accepted.'

A flow chart, *Process for identifying a family after a decision that a child should be placed for adoption*, is reproduced at the end of Chapter 5.

Occasionally, circumstances in the birth family change significantly and there seems a real possibility that a child could live with a family member, even though an adoption plan has been made. In other cases, permanent fostering may come to seem a more realistic option for a child than adoption. Good practice requires that the panel should be notified if the plan has changed.

References

Lord J and Borthwick S (2nd edn) (2008) *Together or Apart? Assessing brothers and sisters for permanent placement*, London: BAAF

Sellick C, Thoburn J and Philpot T (2004) *What Works in Adoption and Foster Care?*, London: Barnardo's

Further reading

Lowe N and Murch M (2002) *The Plan for the Child: Adoption or long-term fostering*, London: BAAF

Neil E and Howe D (eds) (2004) *Contact in Adoption and Permanent Foster Care: Research, theory and practice*, London: BAAF

Ryan T and Walker R (2016) *Life Story Work*, London: CoramBAAF

Schofield G, Beek M and Sargent K with Thoburn J (2000) *Growing up in Foster Care*, London: BAAF

Schofield G and Beek M (2008) *Achieving Permanence in Foster Care*, London: BAAF

Schofield G and Ward E with Warman A, Simmonds J and Butler J (2008) *Permanence in Foster Care: A study of care planning and practice in England and Wales*, London: BAAF

Routes by which a child comes to panel with a proposed adoption plan

Looked after children

Child relinquished for adoption by birth parents

Adoption being requested by birth parents. Other options not appropriate.
↓
Child may be accommodated in foster care.
↓
Statutory counselling of parents about adoption.
↓
Decision to plan for adoption confirmed at review.
↓
Adoption panel for recommendation that child should be placed for adoption.
↓
Agency decision-maker agrees the plan and parents notified.
↓
CAFCASS officer witnesses consent to adoption. (Child at least 6 weeks old.) Child under 6 weeks of age can be placed with adopters with written agreement of birth parent(s).

Birth parent(s) in contact with LA. May be self referral or referral by eg. GP, school, health visitor.
↓
Assessment of child's needs and whether they are being, or could be, met by the birth family, including extended family.
↓
Work with family to enable them to parent their child adequately.
↓
Help may include offering respite care or temporary foster care. This could include placement with relatives. → Child remains at or is returned home.
↓
Case conference/review decision that child should be removed from home or remain looked after. Parents agree.
↓
Child looked after by LA in foster home or children's home under s.20 Ch Act 1989.
↓
Assessment of child's needs. Further work with family. Permanence plan made by review at 4 months. → Return home or special guardianship or long-term fostering.
↓
Decision to plan for adoption confirmed at review. Child may already be subject to a care order made previously. Parents now agree with adoption plan.
↓
Statutory counselling of parents about adoption. They are still in agreement.
↓
Adoption panel for recommendation that child should be placed for adoption.
↓
Agency decision-maker agrees the plan and parents notified.
↓
Parents agree and sign their consent witnessed by CAFCASS – s.19 ACA 2002.

4 Families offering placements

Introduction

The primary purpose of recruiting and approving any family is to meet the needs of children. NMS require the agency 'to implement an effective strategy to recruit and assess prospective adopters who can meet most of the needs of those children for whom adoption is the plan' (NMS 10.1). No particular type of family should be excluded from consideration since the structure of a family does not indicate what the adults' capacity as parents may be. Legislation does not exclude any family structure as inappropriate for children's upbringing. Consideration of parenting abilities does, however, require evidence of the prospective parents' values and attitudes, life experiences, commitment, and flexibility in responding appropriately to individual children. Experience has shown that single people, older people who already have children, gay men and lesbians, people who have remarried, childless couples, and people with disabilities can all have a great deal to offer specific children.

It is important for panels to remember that the great majority of children joining new permanent families will have undergone experiences quite unlike those of most other children in the community. Their new parents will therefore need to have been properly informed and prepared and will need support afterwards.

Guidance 3.10 specifies that: 'The agency should develop a plan for securing sufficient potential adopters who can meet the needs of children waiting for adoption and any children who are likely to need adoption in the future … The agency should consider how prospective adopters might be encouraged and supported to meet any particular needs of children, including older children, disabled children, black and minority ethnic children or children in sibling groups, who they might not have initially considered themselves able to adopt.'

Issues for families seeking intercountry adoption are covered in Chapter 6 since there are issues particular to intercountry adoption over and above those relating to domestic adoption, which need to be carefully considered.

It may be helpful to refer to the flow chart, *Families offering placements*, at the end of this chapter.

Function of the panel

The adoption panel must consider the case of the prospective adopter referred to it by the adoption agency and make a recommendation to the agency as to whether the prospective adopter is suitable to adopt a child. (AAR 26(1))

Where the adoption panel makes a recommendation that the prospective adopter is suitable to adopt a child, the panel may consider and give advice to the agency about the number of children the prospective adopter may be suitable to adopt, their age range, sex, likely needs and backgrounds. (AAR 26(3))

The range of families to be considered

Families being considered at the panel will fall into one of four different categories:

- relatives (or other people significant to the child);
- existing foster carers who now want to adopt;
- prospective adopters who would initially be strangers to the child they are willing to care for. Some of these may have adopted previously or also be considering a Fostering for Adoption (FfA) placement (see p 45); and
- prospective concurrency carers who are seeking dual approval as adopters and foster carers.

Whatever the current status of the family, the great complexity of needs for any child who has been separated from his or her birth parents will have to be addressed. All families offering permanence therefore need to be sensitively and comprehensively assessed irrespective of whether they are existing carers or relatives or a "new" family. Appropriate versions of CoramBAAF's Form PAR* are being developed which can be used for each of these since the assessment involved will in each case require a different perspective.

Relatives or other people significant to the child can offer the unique advantage to the child of maintaining them within their wider family network. This offers greater continuity of family heritage,

---

* The following CoramBAAF forms can be used for assessments: Form PAR (Prospective Adopter's Report) (for concurrent planning/Fostering for Adoption (FFA) carers); Form C (Connected Persons) (for assessing friends and family); Form F Fostering (for assessing foster carers); Form PAR-ICA (for assessing intercountry adopters).

history and relationships. However, the degree of previous contact with the child can vary widely. Research (Sellick *et al*, 2004) has shown that such placements can be very successful. However, there may be particular issues around family dynamics, for example, in cases where relationships with birth parents have been poor or where the child has been sexually abused. The degree of preparation, training and support (including financial) that is available from the agency may play a significant part in both making and maintaining such placements.

Existing approved foster carers can go through a "fast-track" reassessment and approval process which will give due weight to the child's permanence needs. Within this assessment the developmental needs and age of the child, identity issues, cultural and ethnic needs, and the strength and quality of their existing attachments and community links will all play their part.

Guidance 3.81 specifies that: 'It should be made clear to foster carers, or those who apply to be approved for specific children, that their assessment will be in respect of their suitability as adopters generally and that, if they are approved, their suitability to adopt a specific child or children will be addressed separately as part of the matching process.'

New prospective adopters will need assessments that identify clearly their understanding of the likely needs of children and their skills and experience that will enable them to meet these needs. The panel can give advice on the age, sex and the number and likely needs of children for whom the prospective adopter seems best suited.

Adopters who have previously adopted in a court, after having been approved under the AAR 2005 Regulations, can go through a "fast-track" approval process, entering at Stage Two. Guidance 3.75 specifies that 'they should receive a tailored assessment to take account of such factors as their previous experience of adopting or fostering and the needs of the child they have previously adopted/fostered'. Guidance 3.78 states that the agency 'should provide any necessary additional training'. In addition, 'agencies will in each individual case need to determine whether prescribed checks and/or references should be sought depending on the time since approval...' This is left to the agency's discretion, but good practice would suggest that personal referees should be asked for their views and how they think family members will adapt to a new child joining them. Health and police checks have traditionally been updated at least every two years. However, this is not a legal requirement or set out in legislation so agencies should set out their expectations about this in a written policy. From June 2013, with the consent of the person concerned, an online status check can be made to the DBS. This will indicate whether there has been any change since the last check. If there has been a change, a new full police check should be sought from the DBS. Ideally, agencies would encourage applicants to sign up to the update service when their DBS is undertaken in Stage 1. This would allow the agency to check their status at key times such as annual review, matching and application for the adoption order.

Prospective concurrency carers are seeking dual approval as foster carers and adopters. This will enable them to have a child placed under fostering regulations as part of a concurrency scheme. These will be children for whom it is likely that adoption will be the eventual plan. If it is, the child could remain with the carers and be adopted by them, subject to agreement by the court and matching at panel. These carers can be approved as foster carers by the fostering panel or could be approved as adopters and foster carers by an adoption and permanency panel, set up to comply with both sets of regulations (see Chapter 1).

It would be helpful for agency procedures and details of the assessment process in relation to the approval and use of any of these four groups to be added to the folder.

Preparation and assessment process and timescales

Clear timescales are set out, as follows, in guidance. However, 3.46 states that 'where it is clear that Stage One will take longer than two months, for example, because a criminal records check is delayed or the prospective adopter wants more time (they might be struggling with the process or have a significant family bereavement), an agency may delay making their pre-assessment decision. In this case, agencies will be required to detail the reasons for the extended timescale on the prospective adopter's case record, along with supporting evidence.

Effective Adoption Panels

Similarly, Guidance 3.52 states that 'Stage Two should take four months unless there are exceptional circumstances which mean the agency cannot make the decision within that time, or the agency delays making the decision upon the request of the prospective adopter.' Reasons for any extensions should be recorded on the case file. Guidance 3.57 gives the same example for a possible delay as detailed in 3.46.

- General information about adoption should be given to the potential adopters in response to their enquiry.

- The potential adopters should be invited to an adoption information meeting or be offered a pre-planned phone call or an individual interview within **ten days** of their enquiry to an adoption agency.

- Potential adopters will then, if they wish, formally register their interest in proceeding with the agency by completing a **Registration of Interest** form. The agency must decide within **five working days** whether to accept this and to move on to Stage One of the assessment process.

- **Stage One** involves counselling, initial training and preparation, police checks, health checks, references from three individuals and a check with the home local authority. A Stage One written plan must be prepared in consultation with the prospective adopter detailing the work that will be done at this stage. This stage should be completed within **two months**.

- Prospective adopters may, if they wish, take a break after Stage One for a maximum of six months.

- **Stage Two** starts when the agency receives notification from the prospective adopters that they wish to proceed. A Stage Two written assessment plan must be prepared in consultation with the prospective adopter detailing the work to be done, dates for meetings, etc. The work involves an assessment of the prospective adopter's suitability to adopt a looked after child. It ends with the decision-maker's decision about this and should be completed **within four months**.

- Prospective adopters must be given a copy of their PAR (minus references and medical report) and given **five working days** to make comments.

- The agency's decision on whether the prospective adopter should be approved as suitable to adopt should be taken within **seven working days** of receipt of the adoption panel's recommendation and final set of minutes (NMS 17.11).

Information required for a full report

The information required for a full report on a prospective adopter is detailed in the Adoption Agencies (Miscellaneous Amendments) Regulations 2013, Parts 1 and 3 of Schedule 4 and Regulation 30.

Parts 1 and 3 of Schedule 4

- Factual information such as date of birth, ethnicity, religion, etc. A photograph must be obtained.

- Whether he/she is domiciled or habitually resident in the British Islands. (These are England, Wales, Scotland, Channel Islands and the Isle of Man.) To be eligible to adopt in the UK at least one of a couple must be domiciled or both must have been habitually resident for not less than a year at the date of application for an adoption order.

- Personality and interests.

- Details of past relationships and current relationship with partner.

- A family tree.

- A chronology since birth.

- The applicant's observations on his/her experience of being parented and the influence this has had.

- His/her parenting experience and an assessment of his/her parenting ability.

- A description of the wider family, their role and importance in relation to the applicant and to any future child.

- Information on the home, neighbourhood, friendships and social networks.

- Information on household members, including any children, whether living at home or not.

- Educational and employment history and views about how this has influenced them.

- Current employment and how a balance between employment and child care will be achieved.

- Income and expenditure.

- Information on the applicant's capacity to meet a child's needs, share a child's history and understand

and support a child who has feelings of loss and trauma.

- The applicant's reasons for wanting to adopt, views and feelings about adoption, about parenting and his/her capacity to parent, views about a child's education, religious and cultural upbringing and about contact.

- The views of other members of the family, including extended family, about adoption.

- Any other relevant information that might assist the panel or agency.

Regulation 30

- A summary by the agency's medical adviser on the health of the applicants.

- Any relevant information from the area authority reference.

- Any observations in relation to the police checks and arising from preparation groups.

- The agency's assessment of the prospective adopter's suitability to adopt a child.

- Regulations specifically require that the agency must 'in determining the suitability of a couple to adopt a child, have proper regards to the need for stability and permanence in their relationship' (SAR 4(2)). This applies whether or not the couple are married.

- Guidance 3.60 states that 'where there are any issues of significant concern or where clarification is needed', a visit by a team manager or another adoption social worker may be arranged to provide a **second opinion**. However, these visits 'should not be routinely carried out'.

- It will also be helpful if the report describes any adoption support and training needs that have already been identified for the family, with information on how it is planned to meet these.

- The report should describe any discussions which the prospective adopters and the agency workers have had about the range of children, in terms of age, numbers, likely needs and background for whom the prospective adopters would like to be considered. This should include the workers' analysis of their ability to meet the needs of children within this range and should include any difference of view about this between the prospective adopters and the workers.

- Guidance 3.58–59 requires that there is discussion with prospective adopters about whether they may be interested in fostering a child for whom the likely, but not certain, plan is adoption. Such placements are known as **Fostering for Adoption (FFA)**. The agency should indicate in the prospective adopter's report whether they have an interest in FFA. There is no requirement for the panel to consider this information when recommending the suitability of the adopter for approval. However, the 2016 CoramBAAF PAR enables the assessing social worker to cover the information required for approval under Regulation 25a, and as practice has developed in this area, panels have begun to address with applicants their understanding of and preparation for the role of an FFA carer and can then include advice about this to the ADM or nominated officer. The approval of an adopter as an FFA carer is made in relation to a named child and is agreed by a nominated officer, who in many local authorities will also be the ADM, with no further reference to a panel.

- Prospective adopters may also be approved as foster carers to enable them to have a child placed through a concurrency scheme, or to be ready to have a child placed on an FFA basis, before a specific child has been identified. This fostering approval must, in this situation, be done in accordance with fostering regulations by a fostering panel or an adoption and permanence panel. This could be at the same time or not as the approval as prospective adopters.

- The prospective adopter must be shown this report and given five days in which to comment. These comments should be available to the panel.

In addition, the panel should receive:

- a written report on the referee interviews;

- the medical adviser will have the full medical reports but these will not be circulated to each panel member unless so advised by the medical adviser. The panel may, however, request further information which could include some or all of the detailed medical reports.

Checks and references required

See also information on checks and references in Chapter 2.

- **Enhanced police checks from the DBS.** These checks are needed on any member of the household aged 18 or over. The former Glossary to the Guidance stated that "household" 'may include others who do not reside in the home but are considered by the agency to be members of the household as they often stay in or visit the home'.

  Some specified offences automatically exclude applicants. These are mainly offences against children. Panels need to take into account any other offences which may have been committed and consider the implications of these for the adoption of children. Questions to explore include the nature of the offence, the age of the applicant at the time and how long ago this was, the applicant's honesty in disclosing the offence before the police check came in, his or her attitude to the offence now, and whether he or she is still in touch with people who may still be offending. If an applicant has learnt and moved on, their past experience of offending may give them valuable empathy with a child whose birth parents have a history of offending. There is additional information in Chapter 2.

  Applicants may have lived abroad for extended periods. Guidance 3.30 states that the agency 'should decide whether it should carry out any other checks or take up additional references'. It should then decide whether it has sufficient information to justify proceeding with the prospective adopter's application. Some agencies have found that contact with a local police authority in the country concerned has produced helpful information or confirmation that the applicant was not known. An employer's reference covering the period may also be helpful.

- **Any relevant information held by the local authority where the applicants live.** This should include information from children's services records, including child protection, and from education records (Guidance 1.42). It is for agencies to decide whether to get checks from any previous local authorities. Good practice would suggest that the previous ten years should be covered. It may also be helpful to do a check with a local authority where the applicant has jointly parented children with a previous partner.

- **Personal references.** There must be written reports on interviews with at least three personal referees, not more than one of whom may be a relative. It is helpful if, between them, referees have known each applicant for a considerable period of time, as well as still being in close touch. For some applicants, it may be necessary to have information from more than the specified number of referees to achieve this. It can be helpful to have a reference from a relative in each partner's family, rather than from just one side of the family.

- **Former partner and any adult children of either applicant.** It can also be helpful to have a reference from a former partner of either applicant, particularly if there has been joint parenting experience with the applicant. Agencies and panel members need to be clear what their policy is on this. Some ex-partners may be very bitter and angry still, and what they say must be considered in this context. It will be important to try to check any negative comments against the comments of adult children and/or personal referees. Where an applicant refuses to give the information that would allow the agency to contact an ex-partner, particularly if they jointly parented, they should be asked to give reasons for this, e.g. that the ex-partner is violent and might pose a serious threat. As far as possible, these need to be checked against the comments of any adult children or referees. The agency and panel members will then need to make a judgement as to whether the lack of contact with an ex-partner is crucial to the consideration of the applicants or not.

The prospective adopter's report

A report using CoramBAAF's Prospective Adopter's Report (PAR) (including FFA and concurrent placements) (England) should cover all these issues. The report form comes with guidance notes and additional resources and it would be helpful for panel members to have a copy of these. Included in the guidance notes is the comment 'there have been concerns about over-lengthy reports which were repetitive and unfocused, with a lack of analysis of the information...' There is now 'a stronger emphasis on the information being summarised and on the analysis by the social worker undertaking the assessment'.

This is also emphasised in Guidance 3.54 in relation to assessment: 'In conducting the assessment, the social worker should analyse and consider the information they ascertain from and about the prospective adopter, including any issues identified during the adoption preparation. The approach should be objective and enquiring, with information evaluated and its accuracy and consistency checked.'

Long descriptive reports, particularly if based almost exclusively on what prospective adopters have said, are not helpful.

Reports to the adoption panel

The assessing social worker will often share drafts of the report (PAR) with the applicants during the assessment so that they can check it for accuracy and can contribute to it. Once it is completed, Regulation 30 requires that the prospective adopters are given a copy of the report, minus the references and medical report, and invited to make any comments within five working days.

Panel members are then sent:

- the PAR;
- any comments made on it by the prospective adopters;
- written reports of the interviews with referees;
- the medical reports if advised by the medical adviser, but usually a summary by the medical adviser;
- any other relevant information.

Guidance 3.62 clarifies that additional "soft" information obtained from the police cannot be disclosed to the subject or to the panel but must be considered by the agency. If the panel requests additional information, the agency should obtain it, so far as is reasonably practical and Guidance 3.63 makes clear that: 'Unless there is good reason to justify not doing so, additional information...should be shared with the prospective adopter'.

Legal advice

The panel is not required to obtain legal advice but may decide to do so. There could, for example, be issues around domicile and habitual residence or around checks on people who have lived abroad.

Conditional or "in principle" recommendations

Guidance makes clear that the decision-maker's decision must be based on a definite recommendation.

Panel members should ensure that all statutory checks and references are in place and up to date for prospective adopters and that there are no outstanding pieces of information needed. If there are, the panel will need to defer making a recommendation. The agency adviser to the panel is given responsibility (Guidance 1.33) in conjunction, if necessary, with the Chair, to "gatekeep" cases being presented to panel and to withdraw a case prior to panel if important information is missing.

Brief report

The agency does not need to complete a full report where it receives information that leads it to consider that the prospective adopter may not be suitable to adopt a child ((AAR 30(4) and SAR 5)).

This could be information from checks and references or from the health reports or it could be information gathered in the course of interviews by the assessing social worker. Guidance 3.65 specifies that the assessing social worker should seek advice from a manager and they should ensure that the prospective adopter is counselled about the issues of concern. Other professionals should be involved as appropriate, for example, ensuring that health professionals counsel the applicant about information relating to their health.

These discussions should clearly be as open and honest as possible. However, this may not always be possible. There may be concerning information about one applicant, which their partner is unaware of. In this case, the agency may need to give the applicant the choice of telling their partner or of withdrawing, or, after discussion with the applicant concerned, the social worker may need to inform the couple that as a consequence of information obtained from the checks the joint application cannot proceed. Referees may have given concerning information in confidence. If this is the case, the agency should encourage the referee to agree that the concerns can be shared or, if this is not possible, should try and validate the information from other sources.

As a result of these discussions, applicants may decide to withdraw. However, if they do not, and if the agency decides that its concerns will not be alleviated by further work, it must prepare a brief report for panel. Applicants must be shown this report and given five days to comment (AAR 30.5). However, as is the case when a full report is prepared, the health report, references and any additional information, e.g. "soft information" obtained from the police, are not shared.

The panel must consider the report and decide either to request the agency to prepare a full report or to recommend that the prospective adopter is not suitable to adopt a child (AAR 30A). Panel members will need to consider carefully the reasons, which should be detailed in the report, why the agency has taken the view that further work would not resolve the issues.

Given that the social worker and the applicants will not be in agreement on the best outcome, the panel may wish to consider a different process to that usually used. Some panels find it helpful to meet with the applicants first and then, separately, to meet with the social workers.

See later section in this chapter on the decision-making process.

Applicants attending the panel

The agency is required to invite prospective adopters to attend a meeting of the panel when their suitability as adopters is being considered (AAR 30A(5)). Guidance 3.69 states that the purpose is 'to provide an opportunity for both the panel and the prospective adopter to discuss and clarify the prospective adopter's reasons for wishing to adopt, and any other matters that either party considers relevant to the application'. Applicants are not required to attend but it is to be hoped that they will be encouraged to do so. Many panels have virtually 100 per cent attendance by applicants, and both applicants and panel members have found the experience helpful. It is important that prospective adopters are well prepared and given information on who will be present and their roles and also on the panel process.

Applicants may wish to bring a supporter to panel with them. This can be helpful, particularly if the applicant is single. However, it should be made clear to everyone what the support person's role is and whether, for instance, they are permitted to speak. When applicants are in disagreement with the agency, as will be the case when a brief report is presented, it needs to be made clear that the support person, who could be a lawyer, is not there to speak for the applicants. There should be a clear and consistent policy, rather than this being decided on the day.

Many panels formulate their questions and then invite either the social worker in first and then the prospective adopters or both in together. Prospective adopters are usually asked to leave while panel members reach their recommendation. They may be told the recommendation immediately or, less frequently, their social worker may do this later.

It is important that panel members do not let a brief meeting with applicants take the place of a careful consideration of all the issues in the written reports. They need to consider how much weight to give to the attendance and performance of applicants at panel. Some may be much more used than others to talking in a large and fairly formal group. The weight of evidence as to whether people should be recommended for approval should be provided in the written reports. Nevertheless, if people appear very significantly different from the descriptions of them in the reports, this may require more investigation.

Feedback should be gathered from prospective adopters about their experience of attending panel so that the panel can evaluate its performance and make any agreed changes.

CoramBAAF publishes a useful pamphlet entitled *Prospective Adopters Attending Adoption Panel* (Lord, 2016). This is available to buy from CoramBAAF, or is available free to members and member agencies in the members' area of the CoramBAAF website (www.corambaaf.org.uk).

Issues to consider

A family assessment should outline, on the basis of evidence, each family's particular strengths and limitations, the extent to which any concerns are acknowledged or shared by the family itself, and the family's potential for further development.

All family placements involve a careful balancing of the strengths and limitations that exist within each individual family. While the element of risk involved in making family placements for children can never be eliminated, it can be minimised by careful assessment, sound preparation and good support. It is also vital that the panel itself should encourage full acknowledgement, discussion and sharing of the risks involved for a placement, as well as acknowledging the potential demonstrated within each family. This should take place both at the time of considering approval and later, when matching with a child is being considered. All concerns, together with the reasons for these, should be openly voiced and shared. The need for any ongoing work with the family should be identified at the time of approval and the way in which the outcomes of this will be fed back to the panel.

Preparation, training and support

The prospective adopter's report presented to the panel should include details of the content of training already provided by the agency together with unmet training or developmental needs identified, and a clear timetable and plan for meeting these. What further information and support have been available to them pre-placement and what will be available post-placement? All families also need a commitment to continuing to learn about children's needs in the future as knowledge and practice develop. They need to be able to adapt to changes in the child's needs over time and as the child matures.

Strengths needed

The amount of time, energy and space available within each family's emotional and other commitments needs careful consideration. Both the support network and the family's ability to admit difficulties and to use professionals appropriately for support are important. Personal qualities necessary include being able to acknowledge needs from their own and the child's past, not to be rigid or judgemental, to be able to communicate well with children, and to be able to work with the unpredictable. Families should also be able to juggle many demands on their time, energy and resources, acknowledge and value diversity and difference, and be active in the promotion of continuity including a consideration of the child's heritage.

David Quinton, in *Rethinking Matching in Adoptions from Care* (2012), summarised from research the positive aspects of parenting capacity that predicted placement stability were:

- commitment;
- flexible and relaxed approach to parenting;
- realistic expectations;
- ability to distance themselves from the child's behaviour;
- willingness to work with the agency.

Issues relating to the family

Family background and early experience

How has the applicant's early life and relationship with parents, siblings and other significant people influenced the person they are now? Have they been able to talk coherently about the past, however difficult it may have been? Have they been able to build and sustain close relationships and secure attachments? How has their early life influenced the sort of parent they are or plan to be?

Motivation

What is the applicant's motivation? It is important that this is fully explored. Does the family understand its motivation to care for a child? What needs of their own are each of the family members trying to meet? Do they have realistic expectations of themselves? Can they acknowledge needs for support? Have they been encouraged to join any support groups such as Adoption UK (see Appendix IV) or a disability support group if relevant?

Relationship

How long has the couple been together? How stable and permanent does their relationship appear to be? Does either of them have a history of broken relationships? Has the couple weathered any stressful situations together? Regulations stipulate that the agency must consider carefully the 'stability and permanence in their relationship' (SAR 4(2)). Does it have the strength to withstand the demands of an adoption placement?

Unmarried couples can apply jointly for an adoption order. "Couple" is defined in the Adoption and Children Act 2002 section 144(4) as 'a married couple', 'two people who are civil partners of each other' or 'two people (whether of different sexes or the same sex) living as partners in an enduring family relationship'. Section 144(5) of the Adoption and Children Act 2002 spells out that this does not include two people one of whom is the other's parent, grandparent, sister, brother, aunt or uncle.

Infertility issues

Has a couple jointly worked through each partner's own pain and loss? What stage of the grieving process has each reached? Do the adults involved recognise that these feelings may be revived at times throughout their lives? Has each thought about their "fantasy child" and the possible impact of this on a child placed? How would each of them cope if a child were subsequently born to them? If there is no known reason for their infertility, are they prepared to use contraception in the early stages of a child's placement with them?

The guide, *Exploring Infertility Issues in Adoption* (Millar and Paulson-Ellis, 2009) could be helpful.

Health issues

The medical adviser will have a medical report, completed by the applicant's GP, and will have followed up any issues of concern with the GP and with any specialists involved. (The social worker preparing the assessment should liaise with the medical adviser about any health-related issues that come to light during the assessment. Particular care will be needed in handling what may be very sensitive and confidential information.)

The medical adviser should have an up-to-date, holistic and accurate report on the applicant's individual and family health history and current physical, emotional and mental health. This should include lifestyle factors that may have an impact on their ability to parent a vulnerable child. The medical adviser should assist the agency in assessing health and lifestyle risk factors that may affect the decision about the applicant's suitability to care for a child. It is very important that the medical adviser does not see the role as one of accepting or rejecting a particular applicant purely on health grounds. The medical adviser acts as an adviser to the panel, outlining the issues and risks and providing the available evidence base, so that the panel can discuss the case and make a recommendation.

It is important that agencies satisfy themselves that adopters have a reasonable expectation of retaining the health and vigour necessary to meet the physical and emotional needs of a growing child and to care for a child until he or she is grown up. Age is clearly relevant but more significant are specific medical conditions and health-related lifestyle factors such as smoking, alcohol consumption, diet and exercise, as well as looking at what positive factors prospective adopters have to offer a child.

The advice of the medical adviser on health issues will obviously be taken very seriously by other panel members, and eventually, by the agency decision-maker. However, it is important for panel members to be clear that they are jointly responsible for recommendations made to the agency. (See Chapter 2, *Agency policy and practice issues*, for more information on health-related lifestyle factors.) There is helpful additional information in the guide, *Doctors for Children in Public Care* (Mather and Batty, 2000), and in *Promoting the Health of Children in Public Care* (Merredew and Sampeys (eds), 2015).

Other children in the family

How well prepared are such children? Do the adults involved understand the considerable impact there will be on other children in the family? Can they give support to all the children in the family while dealing with conflicting needs or ambivalence from existing children? How well could they deal with difficulties for existing children such as jealousy or aggression towards them or involvement in sexualised behaviour? Research (Sellick *et al*, 2004) indicates that placing a child close in age to an existing birth child adds to the risk of placement breakdown. An age gap of at least two years is usually recommended.

Identity issues

What positive sense does the family have of the sexuality, class, gender, cultural, racial and ethnic, religious and linguistic heritage and identity of its members? Where these are different, how does each member of the family acknowledge and understand and value the diversity represented? What is the social worker's assessment of these issues?

How open would this family be to a child's developing sexuality? In supporting a young person who may be lesbian or gay, what are the potential areas of difficulty the family envisages for itself?

Accommodation, finances and lifestyle

Are there any relevant issues in relation to accommodation and finances? How will the demands of work and child care be managed and what are the financial implications? What are the applicant's current interests and leisure pursuits? Are they prepared for these to change once a child is placed?

Support network

What are the views of family and friends about the adoption plan? Where will support come from? Are the prospective adopters involved in giving support to others, e.g. ageing relatives, and if so, what are the implications for the placement of a child?

The assessment process

Has the process adequately acknowledged and met the needs of all applicants, including those who are single people, those from black and minority ethnic groups, those with disabilities and those who are lesbian or gay? Has the preparation material been appropriate? Have any language or communication needs been suitably addressed? Have any physical requirements been adequately met? Is sufficient understanding and appreciation shown within the assessment of the family's culture, for example, for a deaf family? Has there been any involvement of workers, who are appropriate to this family's needs, within the assessment process?

Discrimination and racism

What understanding and experience do the applicants have of discrimination and racism? What strengths and coping skills do they have? What preparation and support will be available to them? Do they understand and adopt an anti-discriminatory approach to parenting and how is this demonstrated, including within their own family and social networks?

How well will this family be able to help a child placed with them? If they do not share the same ethnicity as the child, Guidance 4.7 states that 'The core issue is what qualities, experiences and attributes the prospective adopter can draw on and their level of understanding of the discrimination and racism the child may be confronted with when growing up'. Does a family that shares the child's ethnicity appreciate the additional tasks they may face, for example, as a result of earlier transracial or transreligious placements, including possible initial rejection by the child? Do single applicants, lesbian or gay applicants, or those with a disability appreciate that significant issues may arise for them because of the child's previous experiences of prejudice and discrimination?

Issues relating to meeting the child's needs

Unidentified needs at time of placement

Does the family realise that some issues may only be identified once the child is in a permanent placement? How will the family cope with areas of unexpected difficulty, for example, medical problems or undisclosed abuse? What support will there be for them?

The child's birth family

All prospective adopters will need to demonstrate understanding of the intense emotional needs of children who have, whatever their age, experienced separation from their birth parents and sometimes from their siblings as well.

Does the family understand and show compassion for the sorts of reasons why children cannot be cared for by their birth parents? Does the family demonstrate insecurity or feelings of ambivalence or rejection towards the varied backgrounds from which a child might come? What do family members feel about a child's family history of mental illness, criminal records, prostitution or alcoholism? Can they identify and value the positive without glossing over any difficulties?

Identifying and understanding the child's wishes and feelings

What importance does the family place on the child's wishes and feelings and how well are family members likely to be able to communicate with the child? Do they understand the pain and loss the child is likely to feel about separation from his or her birth family? Do they accept that, as a result, the child may feel confusion, ambivalence, anger or depression, which may be reflected in his or her behaviour towards new carers? Will they be able to value and continue to help the child with life story work and "retell" the story appropriately as the child matures?

Attachment issues

Does the family acknowledge any limits that a child may show in his or her current ability to form meaningful and positive attachments? Do family members understand the reasons for this? Are their expectations of a child's ability to form new attachments to them realistic? Do they understand the importance of valuing and maintaining in some way links with people with whom the child has good attachments such as grandparents or previous foster carers? Do they understand the special importance of siblings for potential lifetime relationships?

Identity issues

Is there any work that needs to be done with the family before it can fully support and work with the child's sense of identity? Where a transracial placement may be under consideration, how far can the family identify and meet the child's needs and how would they plan to actively fill in any "gaps" they may have in fully meeting the child's needs? What is the family's understanding of how their white identity will impact on their care of a black child? How will they help a black child deal with experiences of racism that they are ultimately unable to share?

Would a child feel comfortable in this family whatever his or her emerging sexuality may be?

Abuse and neglect issues

Does the family understand that they may only learn about some of the child's experiences and needs after placement? What help would family members anticipate giving the child themselves or seeking elsewhere? What future outcome do they expect for a child? Are there any issues in their own background that are relevant and how will they cope with the impact of these?

Behavioural issues

Does the family appreciate the wide range of difficult or disturbed behaviours it may have to cope with? How far do family members understand the impact that the child's previous life experiences will have on both the child and themselves? Is there any evidence of fixed ideas or rigidity around dealing with issues? How important are reward or punishment? How long can they cope when there is no evidence of progress?

Education issues

What is the family's understanding and expectation of children's educational development and the factors that impact on it? Do family members have unresolved issues from their own experiences such as academic expectations that are too high or too low or anxieties about special educational needs? How well could they support a child in difficulty and act as advocates with the school?

Health and disability issues

Disability needs to be considered in terms of the individual child's current development and developmental history, the family's own life experiences, the child's experience of discrimination, and the social context for the child. Can family members advocate for a child by seeking information and resources? Can they promote a child's welfare and independent abilities into adulthood? Can they deal with issues around identity and sexuality? Can they be satisfied with small achievements without underestimating the child's potential for larger ones?

Contact issues

Does the family understand the importance of both identifying and meeting the child's needs for contact, whether direct or indirect? What is their attitude towards contact generally, for example, where and when it should take place, and whether by agreement or court order? Are they open to reassessing and renegotiating a child's needs for contact over time? What support would they need and expect?

The needs of siblings

What understanding does the family show about the needs of siblings? Can family members consider and work with each child as an individual in his or her own right as well as a member of a sibling group? How well could they promote contact and attachment between siblings placed elsewhere, when appropriate? How would they deal with conflicting needs between siblings such as when some have parental contact and others not? Do they have skills, or a willingness to develop these, in working with siblings to promote positive and appropriate relationships with each other?

Range of approval

AAR 30A requires the panel to make a recommendation only about whether a prospective adopter is suitable to be an adoptive parent. However, many prospective adopters wish to be considered for a child or children within a particular age range and with specified needs and they will have been assessed and prepared with these in mind. Panels can give advice to the agency on a specific range of approval. Panel members should clarify whether there is any disagreement between the prospective adopters and the agency workers over the suggested approval range. Panel advice on the approval range 'will inform subsequent matching...but the agency is not restricted by such advice' (Guidance 3.72).

Decision-making process

If, after the panel's recommendation, the decision-maker proposes not to approve the applicants (whether or not this accords with the panel's recommendation), he or she must notify the applicants in writing, giving reasons. This is called a "qualifying determination". If the panel's recommendation was different, i.e. a positive one, the applicants must be told this. The applicants then have 40 working days in which to decide what to do. They can:

- **Accept the proposed decision.** A decision will be made at the end of 40 days or earlier if the applicants confirm in writing that they are withdrawing; OR

- **Make representations to the decision-maker.** He or she will probably receive written information and meet the applicants. He or she can decide whether or not to re-present the case to the panel. If it is, the panel must give the case fresh consideration and make a recommendation and the decision-maker must take this recommendation into account when making the decision, which is final; OR

- **Apply to the Independent Review Mechanism– Adoption and Fostering (IRM).** This has been operating since April 2004 in relation to adoption and was extended, from April 2009, to include fostering. It is an independent review process, conducted by a panel. Prospective or approved adopters and foster carers may apply to the IRM, following a "qualifying determination" made on the basis of a full, or in the case of adopters only, a brief, report. They will be invited to attend an independent panel, set up in a similar way to an agency panel. The agency will send representatives to the panel too. The IRM panel will receive all the reports presented to the agency's panel and may request some additional information. It will not have a copy of the panel minutes. Its recommendation and minutes will go to the agency decision-maker, who will make the final decision. Further information about the IRM, including details of number of cases heard, decisions made and reasons for these, can be found at www.independentreviewmechanism.org.uk/.

Review and termination of approval

Regulations require agencies to review the approval of prospective adopters until a child is placed. This must be done 'whenever the adoption agency considers it necessary' but otherwise at least annually (AAR 30D).

Where the agency completes its review and considers that the prospective adopter remain suitable to adopt, it need only inform the prospective adopter and record its view on the prospective adopter's case record. In the case of intercountry adopters, the outcome should also be notified to the Department's intercountry adoption casework team. (Guidance 3.90)

The case only needs to be referred to the panel if the agency proposes to terminate approval. If this is the case, it must prepare a report giving its reasons. The prospective adopter must be given 10 days to comment on this before it goes to the panel. The prospective adopter must be invited to attend panel (Guidance 3.69). The panel makes a recommendation, having requested further information if required. The decision-making process is then as already described, with the prospective adopter having the right to apply to the IRM.

In addition to carrying out a review annually, a review should be held if the agency has serious concerns about the prospective adopters and also after any significant event, such as a couple separating, a new health issue, a pregnancy or a disrupted placement.

Effective Adoption Panels

Families offering placements – from first enquiry to approval

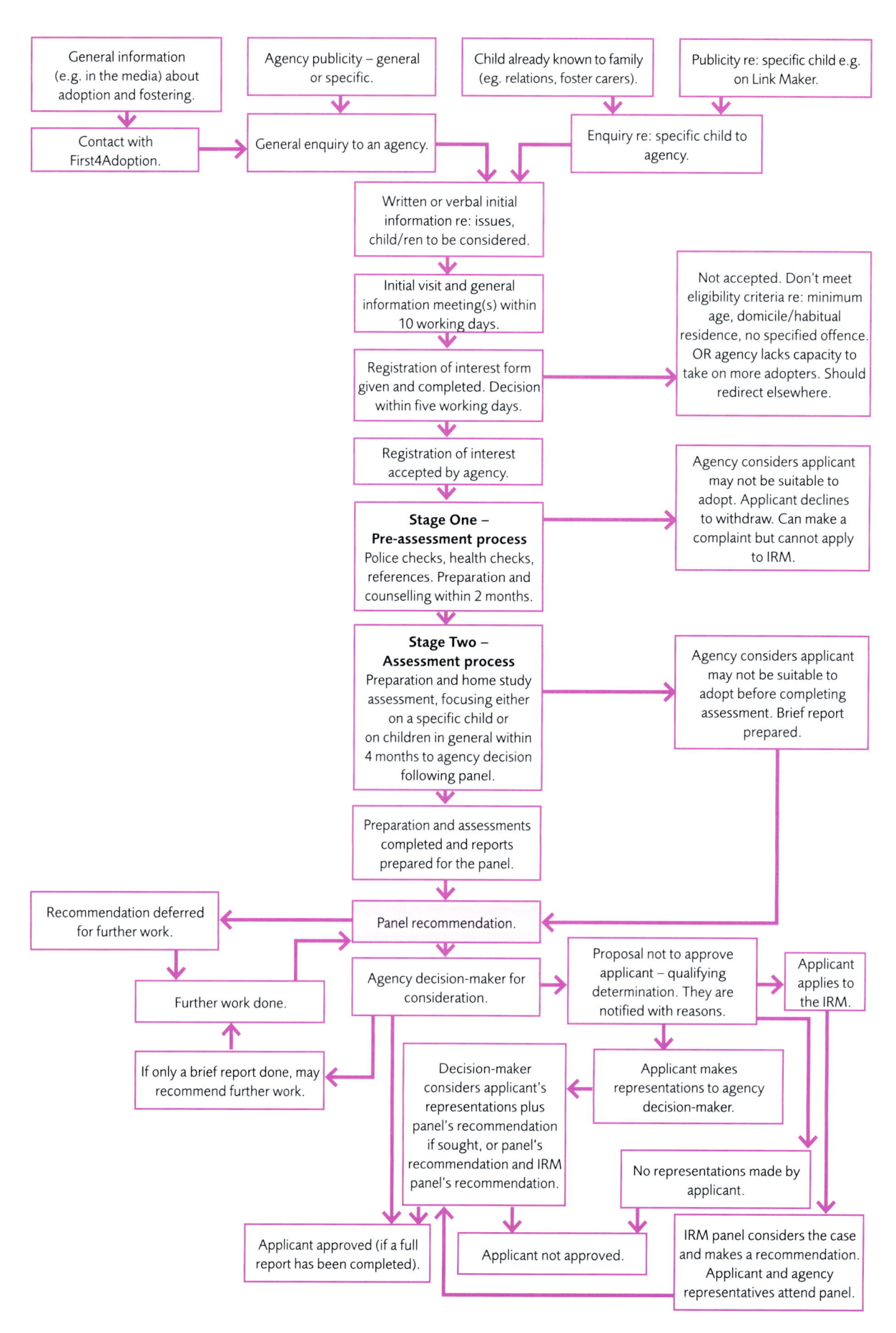

```
[General information (e.g. in the media) about adoption and fostering.]
    ↓
[Contact with First4Adoption.] → [General enquiry to an agency.] ← [Agency publicity – general or specific.]
                                        ↑
[Child already known to family (eg. relations, foster carers).] → [Enquiry re: specific child to agency.] ← [Publicity re: specific child e.g. on Link Maker.]
                                        ↓
[Written or verbal initial information re: issues, child/ren to be considered.]
    ↓
[Initial visit and general information meeting(s) within 10 working days.]
    ↓
[Registration of interest form given and completed. Decision within five working days.] → [Not accepted. Don't meet eligibility criteria re: minimum age, domicile/habitual residence, no specified offence. OR agency lacks capacity to take on more adopters. Should redirect elsewhere.]
    ↓
[Registration of interest accepted by agency.]
    ↓
[Stage One – Pre-assessment process: Police checks, health checks, references. Preparation and counselling within 2 months.] → [Agency considers applicant may not be suitable to adopt. Applicant declines to withdraw. Can make a complaint but cannot apply to IRM.]
    ↓
[Stage Two – Assessment process: Preparation and home study assessment, focusing either on a specific child or on children in general within 4 months to agency decision following panel.] → [Agency considers applicant may not be suitable to adopt before completing assessment. Brief report prepared.]
    ↓
[Preparation and assessments completed and reports prepared for the panel.]
    ↓
[Recommendation deferred for further work.] ← [Panel recommendation.]
    ↓                                              ↓
[Further work done.]                         [Agency decision-maker for consideration.] → [Proposal not to approve applicant – qualifying determination. They are notified with reasons.] → [Applicant applies to the IRM.]
    ↑                                              ↓                                                      ↓
[If only a brief report done, may recommend further work.] ← [Decision-maker considers applicant's representations plus panel's recommendation if sought, or panel's recommendation and IRM panel's recommendation.] ← [Applicant makes representations to agency decision-maker.]
                                                                                                                 ↓
                                                                                                          [No representations made by applicant.]
    ↓                                         ↓                                                                  ↓
[Applicant approved (if a full report has been completed).]   [Applicant not approved.]   [IRM panel considers the case and makes a recommendation. Applicant and agency representatives attend panel.]
```

What next?

A panel recommends that applicants are suitable to be adoptive parents and the agency makes a decision about this. The panel may then not hear about the prospective adopters again until a matching with a child is presented. These matches are usually presented to the panel of the child's agency and so a voluntary adoption agency panel may have no further involvement after its initial recommendation.

Once the agency has approved the adopter, it must prepare a written matching plan in consultation with him or her. This should set out the process for making a placement and for subsequent reviews. It should also cover how a child will be identified and the prospective adopter's role in this and information about making representations. AAR 30G requires that the prospective adopter is referred to the Adoption Register as soon as possible, and within no more than three months, unless a specific child is being actively considered for placement.

It is important that agency staff have regular contact with approved adopters who are waiting to be matched with a child. Panels should receive regular brief updating reports, perhaps every three or six months, which would give the conclusion of reviews and detail any changes made to advised approval ranges. They should check on whether families have been referred to the Adoption Register and be put in touch with Adoption UK, the self-help group for adoptive and prospective adoptive parents (see Appendix IV).

References

Lord J (2016, 2nd edn) *Prospective Adopters Attending Adoption Panel*, London: CoramBAAF

Mather M and Batty D (2000) *Doctors for Children in Public Care: A resource guide advocating, protecting and promoting health*, London: BAAF

Merredew F and Sampeys C (eds) (2015) *Promoting the Health of Children in Public Care*, London: BAAF

Millar I and Paulson-Ellis C (2009) *Exploring Infertility Issues in Adoption*, London: BAAF

Sellick C, Thoburn J and Philpot T (2004) *What Works in Adoption and Foster Care?*, London: Barnardo's/BAAF

5 Matching children with families

Panel functions

Regulation 32 of the Adoption Agencies Regulations 2005 requires the panel to consider and to recommend 'whether the child should be placed for adoption with that particular prospective adopter'.

It must also consider and may give advice to the agency about:

(a) the authority's proposals for the provision of adoption support services for the adoptive family;

(b) the arrangements the adoption agency proposes to make for allowing any person contact with the child; and

(c) whether the parental responsibility of any parent or guardian or the prospective adopter should be restricted and, if so, the extent of any such restriction.

The panel must have regard to the duties imposed by section 1 of the Adoption and Children Act 2005 ("the welfare checklist") when considering its recommendation. See Chapter 2 for information on this.

The decisions about the adoption plan for the child and about the suitability of the prospective adopters will probably already have been made. However, one or both of those recommendations can be made at the same time as the matching recommendation (AAR 32 and Guidance 4.33).

Matching considerations draw very heavily on the work that will have been done already in identifying a child's needs and deciding on a plan and in assessing and preparing a family and identifying their strengths and limitations. It will probably be helpful, therefore, to refer back to Chapters 3 and 4, *Considering adoption for a child* and *Families offering placements*.

The flow chart at the end of this chapter, *Process for identifying a family and making a match after a decision that a child should be placed for adoption*, might also be helpful.

Process by which the proposed match has reached the panel

Proposed matches are made in a variety of ways:

- The family may have been identified from the agency's own waiting list of approved families.

- A link may have been made with a family already approved by another agency. This could have been done by referral to the local consortium to which the agency belongs, by referral to one of the Adoption Registers (the Adoption Register in England, Wales Adoption Register, Scotland's Adoption Register or the Adoption Regional Information System Northern Ireland (ARIS)), or by referral to a family-finding service such as Adoption UK's Children who Wait, or Link Maker. There may have been direct contact with other agencies or the child's need for a family may have been publicised in national media.

- The family may have been recruited and assessed with this specific child in mind, probably by responding to publicity for the child before they had started the assessment process.

- The family may be the child's current foster carers:
  - either foster carers who later decided to adopt and have been assessed as adopters; or
  - concurrent carers who were approved to adopt as well as foster from the start; or
  - Fostering For Adoption carers who are adopters who have been approved as temporary foster carers for this specific child.

- The family may know the child in some other way, for example, as a family member or as a friend or a teacher. They will have been assessed and approved with this particular child in mind.

The child's social worker may have had more than one family to consider. He or she will have read their reports and met the families and their workers, often with the adoption worker who is family finding for the child. The child's foster carer or residential social worker may well have met the families too. Those involved will have considered what each family has to offer to this particular child and their potential to provide a stable and permanent family for him or her. Guidance 4.22 makes it clear that: 'The agency is responsible for considering and comparing alternative prospective adopters for a particular child. In its report to the panel on the proposed placement, the agency should only propose one adoptive family (that is, one couple or a single person) as the prospective adopter(s).'

Matching children with families

Research indicates that there may be a poorer outcome if the matching decision has been taken informally rather than through a formal matching meeting and panel members could ask about this.

AAR 31 requires that, when the agency has decided which family to proceed with, they must give them a copy of the child's permanence report and any other relevant information. This could include photos and a video of the child. They must then meet with the prospective adopters and ascertain their views on the placement and on the proposed arrangements for ongoing contact with members of the birth family or others.

If the agency and the adopters are then keen to proceed with a match, the agency must carry out an assessment of the needs of the child, the prospective adopters and any other children whom they may have, for adoption support services. A copy of the Adoption Passport, written to inform prospective adopters about support and how to access it, is available at www.first4adoption.org.uk/adoption-support/the-adoption-passport/.

Timescales

Guidance 4.2 specifies that:

The following timescales apply where the agency proposes to place a child with the prospective adopter, whether the prospective adopter is resident in the UK or abroad:

- *a proposed placement with a suitable prospective adopter should be identified and approved by the panel within **six months** of the agency deciding that the child should be placed for adoption;*

- *where a parent has requested that a child aged under six months be placed for adoption, a proposed placement with a suitable prospective adopter should be identified and approved by the panel within **three months** of the agency deciding that the child should be placed for adoption;*

- *the agency's decision on whether to approve a proposed placement with a suitable prospective adopter should be taken within **seven working days** of the receipt of the adoption panel's recommendation and final set of panel minutes.* (NMS 17.11)

Guidance is clear that, although these timescales should generally be adhered to, the paramount consideration must always be the welfare of the child. Where the agency is unable to comply with a timescale or decides not to, the reasons for this should be recorded on the child's case record.

AAR 32(5) allows a panel to make a matching recommendation at the same panel meeting as recommends the plan for the child and the approval of the adopter. However, usually this will already have been done.

Authorisation to place for adoption

Before a child can be placed for adoption the agency must have one of the following:

- a placement order made by a court;
- formal consent from the birth parent(s) witnessed by a CAFCASS officer;
- agreement by the birth parent(s) to place an infant under the age of six weeks. There is a prescribed form for this written agreement at the end of Chapter 2 of the Guidance. The parent(s) should give formal consent as soon as possible after the child is six weeks old.

Panel members should ensure that at least one of these is in place or is planned. A placement order can be made if the grounds for making a care order are met or if the child has no parent or guardian. The court can simply make a placement order. However, in most cases it will be better if it first makes a care order. This will be suspended while the placement order is in force, but will be reinstated should the placement order be revoked before the child is adopted.

Formal consent to placement for adoption can only be given once a child is at least six weeks old. This can be consent to placement with identified adopters, consent to placement with any adopters chosen by the agency or consent to the latter should the child be removed from or returned by the identified adopters.

Child already living with the family

The child may already be living with the family as a foster child. They may be relatives or temporary foster carers who have decided to adopt, or they may be concurrent carers or Fostering for Adoption carers who have had the possibility of adoption in mind from the start of the placement. The panel will have the advantage of social work reports and comments from the carers about relationships in the family and about the quality of the placement. However, as Practice Guidance for Fostering for Adoption states, 'its role is still to make a recommendation about a placement that is fundamentally changing its legal and psycho-social status from foster care to adoption. In that sense the role of the panel is not to "rubber stamp" that which has already happened but to openly and supportively explore what has happened and what might need to happen.'

Many relatives wanting to offer permanence to a child in their family will do so with a special guardianship order. However, Guidance 4.14 states that 'there may be some circumstances where the security provided by the irrevocability of an adoption order and its lifelong effect, would be best for the child and outweigh the potential drawbacks of the "skewing" of relationships. For example, a grandparent adopting their grandchild would be legally the child's parent... There is no presumption that a special guardianship order would be preferable to an adoption order if the placement is with a relative.' Case law supports this and emphasises that each case must be considered on its own facts.

Information required

Panel members should expect to have up-to-date and fully completed copies of the following reports.

On the child

- **A copy of the child's permanence report:** This should include updated information as necessary to ensure that it gives an accurate account of the current situation.

- The CPR will include a health summary by the medical adviser and he or she will also have the full health reports available on the child and birth family members. Other panel members are entitled to see these if they wish.

- Possibly other relevant specialist reports to ensure a comprehensive picture of the child's needs.

- Minutes of the panel meeting that recommended that the child should be placed for adoption, including any advice on contact arrangements.

On the family

- **The prospective adopter's report (CoramBAAF's Form PAR can be used).**

- The PAR will include a summary by the medical adviser of the adopter's health (CoramBAAF's Form AH can be used). He or she will also have full medical reports available. In most cases, Form AH should remain valid for two years. However, CoramBAAF recommends that medical advisers telephone the GP for an informal update if a child is to be placed more than six months after the prospective adopter's medical examination.

- Minutes of the panel meeting that recommended approval and the panel's advice on approval range. It should be noted that Guidance 3.72 comments that research indicates that "stretching" of the adopter's preferences puts placements at higher risk of difficulties.

If the proposed match does not reflect the advice of the approval panel or the decision-maker on the range of approval, panel members could ask about the reasons for this and about the work done by the adopters and the agency to expand the range. The CoramBAAF Form APR 2016 asks for this updating information to be provided as part of the APR (see below).

The adoption placement report

AAR 31 requires that an adoption placement report is written (CoramBAAF's Form APR 2016 can be used), to include the following:

- The agency's reasons for proposing the placement.

- The views of the prospective adopter about the proposed placement and the proposed arrangements for contact with birth relatives or others.

- The agency's proposals for the provision of adoption support services to the adoptive family. (Where the agency is a voluntary adoption agency, it is recommended that it seeks, and includes in the report, any proposals the relevant local authority may have.)

- The arrangements the agency proposes to make for allowing any person contact with the child.

The prospective adopter must have been given a copy of the child's permanence report to read, plus any other information that the agency considers relevant. Proposed contact arrangements must have been discussed with them, and there must also have been an assessment of the adoption support needs of the family. Guidance 4.24 makes clear that: 'It is unacceptable for agencies to withhold information about a child and provide a picture that bears little relation to the reality'.

The prospective adopter must also have been given a copy of the placement report and ten days in which to comment, before the reports go to panel. Any comments made, if not incorporated into the report, should be given to panel.

It can also be helpful to have a brief summary of how family finding was done, how this particular family was found, and whether any other families were considered.

Guidance 4.25 states that: 'It is good practice for the medical adviser to meet with the prospective adopter to share all appropriate health information, to discuss the needs of the children…and to provide a written report of this meeting'.

Legal advice

The panel is not required to obtain legal advice for a matching but may do so. Legal factors may have changed since the plan for the child was considered. For example, birth parents might now have a different attitude to the adoption plan or different wishes about contact.

Attendance at the panel

The child's worker, and if possible his or her manager, and the family's worker should be present. It may also be helpful if the child's carer can attend for part of the discussion. Prospective adopters should also be invited to attend panel. It may be particularly helpful to discuss with them their views on proposed adoption support arrangements, on contact, and on the exercise of their parental responsibility for the child after placement.

It is not usual for either the child or his or her birth parents to attend. However, it is important that panel members are fully informed about their views and wishes in relation to adoptive families in general and to this particular family if they have information

about them. They could be invited to write or send an audiotape to panel members or to the Chair, if they wish.

Welfare of children

The panel, like the agency, is bound by the duties set out in section 1 of the Adoption and Children Act 2002. This is given in full in Chapter 2, and should be the overarching context in which the match for a child is considered.

Issues to consider

The art of making permanent placements appears to be in learning what the new parents have to give and what they will expect in return, and matching these with what the child needs and is willing to take from the new parents, and also what the child can give back to them. (Sellick and Thoburn, 1996)

No match will be "perfect" and panel members need to clarify and weigh up the risks and limitations as well as the strengths of the proposed match and to consider the adoption support services being proposed post-placement to try and minimise the risks.

The following list indicates some of the issues that panel members will need to consider. It is not intended to be exhaustive and other issues will need to be addressed in individual cases. Panel members should remember that they are not re-considering the approval of the family; they are considering whether the family can meet the needs of this particular child or sibling group.

The child's birth family

Panel members will need to check whether there have been any significant changes in the views or circumstances of birth family members since the plan for the child was made. Are there any particular factors, for example, the mental illness of a parent, which the prospective adopters may find difficult to accept? Is the family able to understand and accept the child's history?

In appropriate circumstances the proposed placement will…have been discussed with the child's birth family and their views should be included in the [placement] report. (Guidance 4.29)

The child's current understanding of and feelings about the past and about what is planned

Panel members will need to ask about the progress of the direct work that is being done with the child and about how ready the child is to move to a new family. How long has the child been waiting and how has he or she coped with this? Do the prospective adopters understand that the child will probably continue to need help for a long time to make sense of what has happened and to sort out his or her feelings toward their birth family? How able will the family be to help the child with this and what outside support will be available? What sort of family is the child envisaging? If this family is different, for example, a single parent when the child has assumed that he or she will have two parents, what work is being done to prepare the child?

The views of the child about the proposed placement are not required to be included in the placement report but 'where this has been discussed with the child, and particularly where the child already knows the prospective adopter (perhaps as their current foster carer), this will be relevant information to be included in the report' (Guidance 4.29).

Identity issues

The Children and Families Act 2015 introduced changes to the responsibility placed on agencies to consider the cultural, ethnic, religious and linguistic background of the child when achieving a match, as set out in Draft Guidance (2014) 3.5.

Section 1(5) of the Act has been repealed to ensure that in placing a child for adoption, differences in ethnicity, religion, culture or language are not given such undue emphasis or prominence that they result in potential placements not being explored or an otherwise satisfactory adoption placement not going ahead. This is particularly important when black children wait a year longer to be adopted than white children, and some children simply grow out of the chance of adoption.

The 2014 Guidance 3.4 sets out that:

A prospective adopter can be matched with a child with whom they do not share the same ethnicity, if they can respect, reflect or actively develop a child's racial identity from the point they are matched and as they develop throughout their childhood. The Government is clear that a black, Asian or mixed ethnicity prospective adopter can be a successful adopter of a white or mixed ethnicity child and a white prospective adopter can be a successful adopter of a child who is black, Asian or of mixed ethnicity.

3.7 It is important that when social workers are looking for an adoptive family for a child, that they avoid placing the child's ethnicity above other characteristics without strong, well analysed reasons for doing so. An ethnic match is an advantage in an adoption but that is just one of a large number of considerations to be taken account of when matching prospective adopters and children. In practice, ethnicity has frequently been given undue significance in matching.

3.8 What matters in the matching of a child with a prospective adopter of differing ethnicity are the qualities, experiences and attributes the prospective adopter can draw on and their level of understanding of how discrimination and racism operates in society at both an individual and an institutional level. It is therefore vital that the prospective adopter has the openness, strength and insight to support the child or young person if they are confronted by racism when growing up. When such characteristics are present in a prospective adopter the placements can be made with confidence.

Where the proposed new parents are not of the same cultural, ethnic, religious and linguistic background as the child, panel members will therefore need to ask what efforts have been made to find such a family, and whether, with appropriate support, the family can nevertheless meet the child's needs. Does the family live in an ethnically diverse area? Do they have family members or friends of the same ethnicity as the child? If the proposed placement is to be recommended, what efforts are to be made by the family and the agency to actively meet the child's needs?

Attachment issues

It will be very important for panel members to try and assess whether the proposed family has understood the long-term implications for the child and for his or her relationship with them of the child's early attachment experience. Does the family have realistic expectations of the child's ability to make an attachment to them?

Abuse and neglect issues

Does the family understand that the child may well have experienced more abuse than is currently known about? Are family members prepared, for instance, for the child to disclose previous sexual abuse once they are settled in their new family? Are there any issues in the family members' own backgrounds that are relevant here and how will they cope with the impact of these?

Behavioural issues

It will be helpful for panel members to check whether the proposed family has met the child's current carers to hear first hand about what the child is like to live with. Is there any aspect of the child's behaviour that is likely to be particularly difficult for the new family? Is their approach to parenting and to discipline very different from that which the child is used to? How will they deal with the child's possible confusion about this?

Health and disability issues

The medical adviser will be able to discuss with other panel members issues relating to the health of the child and of their birth parents, and the implications of these for the proposed placement. The medical adviser may have already discussed these issues with the proposed adopters. Panel members will need to be sure that the prospective adopters understand the implications of uncertainties or gaps in the health information as well as of known factors. The medical adviser will be able to discuss with other panel members any health or disability issues in the prospective adoptive family and the implications of these for the particular child being matched. The medical adviser will also be able to outline the services that are likely to be needed to meet the child's health and disability needs in the future.

Education issues

Panel members will need to be clear that the prospective adopters have been given information about and understand the educational needs of the child. It will be helpful for the adopters to meet with the child's teachers and panel members should check whether this has already happened or is planned after the formal matching. Are there any particular factors in this child's educational needs that may be difficult for this family to meet? What are the facilities in their area and are any necessary specialist resources available?

The needs of siblings

It will be important to consider whether the proposed placement seems likely to meet the particular needs of each sibling in the group. Guidance 4.12 states that: 'Siblings should be adopted by the same prospective adopter unless there is good reason why they should not be. Where an agency is making a placement decision on two or more children from the same family it should be based on a comprehensive assessment of the quality of the children's relationship, their individual needs and the likely capacity of the prospective adopter to meet the needs of the siblings being placed together.'

Other children in the new family

Research (quoted in Sellick and Thoburn, 2004) indicates that it is risky to place children too close in age to existing children in a family. Proposed matches with small age gaps will need to be carefully considered. Are there particular factors about the needs of the existing children and the needs of the child to be placed that are likely to be incompatible?

The family's feelings and expectations

It may be helpful if panel members ask why the family feels that they would be right for this particular child and that this particular child would be right for them. What are each family member's expectations of how the child will fit into their family and relate to them? Does this match with what is known about the child's needs and wishes and capacity to form relationships?

Adoption support services

The adoption placement report must include the local authority's proposals for providing adoption support services to the adoptive family and the adoption panel is required to consider these. (If the family has been approved by a voluntary adoption agency, the adoption support that this agency will offer should also be described.) The panel should also have any comments that the prospective adopters have made on the proposals. The placing local authority is responsible for assessing for and arranging the provision of adoption support services for three years

Effective Adoption Panels

after the adoption order. Any regular financial support agreed before the adoption order is made remains their responsibility long term.

Adoption support services are likely to be crucial to the success of the placement. There will almost certainly be some limitations and risks in any match as well as strengths, and panel members will need to check on the particular help that is planned to compensate in these areas. What help and support are proposed, and from whom, both after placement and after adoption? It is particularly important to check on this in interagency placements and in cases when the family may live outside the child's home area. What is the family's attitude to seeking help and to working with others, for instance, specialist therapists, whose help the child may need? Are the agency and family aware that support and help may be needed in the future even though this is not apparent at the time of placement? How will a need for help in the future be met? Panel members should check on the availability of specialist educational and medical facilities that may be necessary. The medical adviser will have a continuing role until the child is adopted and this can be helpful. Is a prospective adopter planning to give up work or take extended leave? What is the likely impact on the family of this?

Financial issues

These must be considered as part of adoption support services.

ASR 8 sets out the circumstances in which financial support may be paid to an adoptive parent. These include:

(a) *where it is necessary to ensure that the adoptive parent can look after the child;*

(b) *where the child needs special care which requires greater expenditure of resources by reason of illness, disability, emotional or behavioural difficulties or the continuing consequences of past abuse or neglect;*

(c) *where it is necessary for the local authority to make any special arrangements to facilitate the placement or the adoption by reason of*

  – *the age or ethnic origin of the child*

  – *the desirability of the child being placed with the same adoptive parents as his brother or sister (whether of full or half-blood) or with a child with whom he previously shared a home;*

(d) *where such support is to meet the recurring costs in respect of travel for the purpose of visits between the child and a related person.*

The support given cannot normally include remuneration. However, **foster carers who apply to adopt a child in their care** can continue to be paid any remuneration they received. This remuneration element will usually cease to be paid from two years after the adoption order 'unless the local authority considers its continuation to be necessary having regard to the exceptional needs of the child or any other exceptional circumstances' (ASR 9).

There must usually be an assessment of the prospective adopter's means before financial support is agreed. However, the local authority *may* disregard means in the situations outlined in b), c) and d) above, when considering the payment of remuneration to a former foster carer, as described above, and when considering the initial costs of accommodating an agency adoptive child – a "settling-in grant".

Contact arrangements

The adoption placement report must include the agency's proposals for allowing any person contact with the child and the panel is required to consider these. The panel should also have any comments made by the prospective adopter.

Panel members should note that AAR 45(2) removes the general duty in the 1989 Children Act to promote contact. When an agency is authorised to place a child for adoption,

... there should be no general presumption for or against contact. This is why Regulation 45.2 of the Adoption Agencies Regulations 2005 (AAR) removes the general duty in the 1989 Act to promote contact. Contact between adopted children and their birth families can be beneficial, but research has also highlighted that any form of contact needs careful planning and support, and that children's views and their needs for contact may change over time so any contact plans must be kept under review. (Guidance 7.1 and 7.2)

Contact with birth family members and other people significant to the child after placement can be contentious and panel members should clarify the child's needs for ongoing contact and the proposed family's willingness and ability to meet these needs. What actual contact is planned and with whom? A child's need for contact will probably change over time, and the family's flexibility on this should be clarified. What help and support will the agency give over managing contact? Will agency workers be available to help renegotiate contact in the future if this becomes necessary?

Contact after placement may be through letters and cards exchanged via the adoption agency by the adoptive family and birth family members or there may be face-to-face contact. Contact arrangements need to be considered not only for birth parents but for grandparents and other relatives and for siblings placed elsewhere (AAR 46 and 47 and Guidance Chapter 7 deal with contact). Panel members should be aware that the Children and Families Act 2014 introduced section 51A, that enables the court to make a contact order or a no contact order at the point of the adoption order being made and to identify with the social workers where this might be appropriate.

Parental responsibility

The panel must consider and may give advice to the agency about whether the parental responsibility of any parent or guardian or the prospective adopter should be restricted, and if so, the extent of any such restriction.

For the first time, under the Adoption and Children Act 2002, adoptive parents are given parental responsibility for the child on placement, rather than on the making of the adoption order, as before. They share this with the local authority and with any birth parent or guardian who has parental responsibility. The local authority has the power to restrict the parental responsibility of any parent, guardian or prospective adopter.

It will be helpful if the agency includes in the adoption placement report its proposals, if any, for any restrictions. It is likely that the exercise of parental responsibility by any parent or guardian has already been considerably restricted and will probably be even more so once the child is placed for adoption, although they will not lose it until the child is adopted. In coming to a view on any restriction on the prospective adopter's exercise of their parental responsibility, the agency and the panel should take account of the views of the prospective adopter, of the child, if he or she is of sufficient age and understanding, and of anybody else, which could include the birth parents or other relatives. Guidance 5.20 suggests that: 'It may well be appropriate for there to be a gradual "shift of power" so that the prospective adopter comes to have a greater degree of autonomy as the placement progresses and their confidence and parenting skills develop, bearing in mind that once the adoption order is made they alone will have parental responsibility'.

Baby placements where the child is relinquished for adoption

Birth parents are not able to consent formally to adoption until an infant is at least six weeks old. However, a baby younger than this can be placed for adoption provided the parent(s) have given their agreement to this in writing (AAR 35(3), (4)). There is a prescribed form for this agreement at the end of Guidance Chapter 2. Once the baby is six weeks old, the agency must arrange for the parent(s)' formal consent to adoption, under section 19 of the Adoption and Children Act 2002. The consent, on a prescribed form, must be witnessed by a CAFCASS officer.

Guidance 2.46 suggests that, when parents have been counselled and adoption is considered the preferred adoption, the agency should start work on the permanence report and the health report. It should:

... arrange for the agency medical adviser and adoption panel to be ready to consider the case as soon as possible after the child is born...with enough preparation the adoption panel should be ready to consider the case within a day or so of the birth.

A placement before the child is six weeks old should only be made following further counselling of the parent(s) after the birth. Adoptive parents will need to be well prepared for the risk of the parent(s) changing their minds before the child is six weeks old, in which case the baby would return to them (unless there were grounds for care proceedings). They will also need to be prepared for health issues to emerge

Effective Adoption Panels

Process for identifying a family after a decision that a child should be placed for adoption

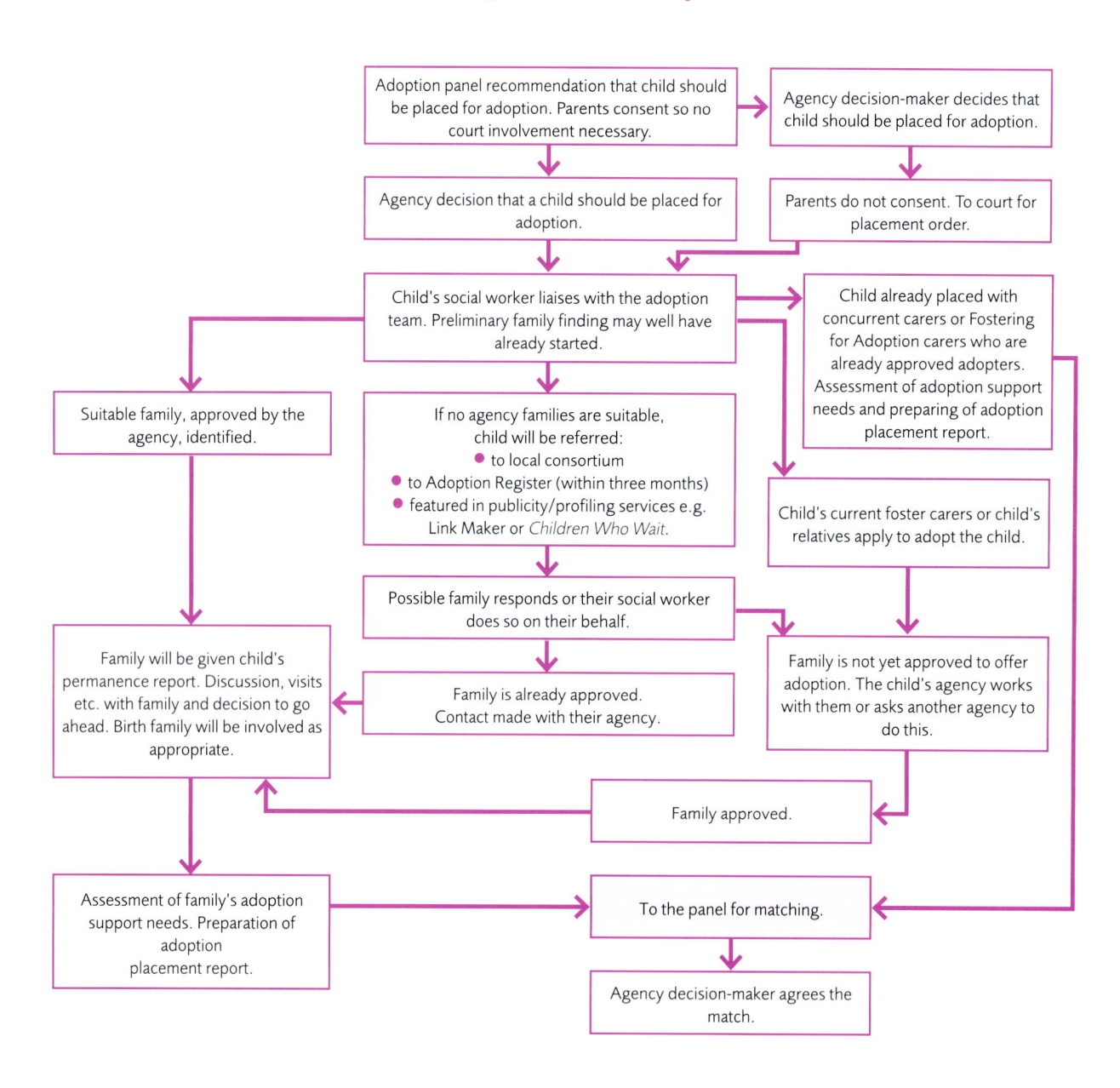

```
Adoption panel recommendation that child should        Agency decision-maker decides that
be placed for adoption. Parents consent so no    →     child should be placed for adoption.
         court involvement necessary.
                    ↓                                              ↓
  Agency decision that a child should be placed for      Parents do not consent. To court for
                   adoption.                                    placement order.
                    ↓                    ↓ ←─────────────────────┘
     Child's social worker liaises with the adoption    →    Child already placed with
     team. Preliminary family finding may well have          concurrent carers or Fostering
                   already started.                          for Adoption carers who are
                    ↓                                        already approved adopters.
                                                             Assessment of adoption support
                                                             needs and preparing of adoption
                                                             placement report.
                    ↓
          If no agency families are suitable,
                child will be referred:
                • to local consortium                   Child's current foster carers or child's
                • to Adoption Register (within three months)   relatives apply to adopt the child.
                • featured in publicity/profiling services e.g.
                  Link Maker or Children Who Wait.
                    ↓                                              ↓
       Possible family responds or their social worker    Family is not yet approved to offer
             does so on their behalf.                     adoption. The child's agency works
                    ↓                                     with them or asks another agency to
              Family is already approved.                             do this.
              Contact made with their agency.
                                                                    ↓
    Suitable family, approved by the                         Family approved.
              agency, identified.
                    ↓
       Family will be given child's
    permanence report. Discussion, visits
    etc. with family and decision to go
    ahead. Birth family will be involved as
                appropriate.
                    ↓
     Assessment of family's adoption          →       To the panel for matching.       ←
       support needs. Preparation of
                adoption
             placement report.
                                                                    ↓
                                                    Agency decision-maker agrees the
                                                                 match.
```

64

as the infant develops. However, if prospective adopters are prepared to take these risks, the benefit to the infant of a very early placement could be considerable. There is useful discussion of these issues in the Good Practice Guide *Right from the Start: Best practice in adoption planning for babies* (Cousins, 2003).

Reaching a recommendation on a proposed match

As described earlier, prospective adopters will have been given quite a lot of information about the child. They may have met the foster carers, their adoption support needs will have been assessed, and they may, for example, have visited possible schools. The match can feel like a fait accompli. However, panel members have a responsibility to make a recommendation with, as always, the child's welfare throughout his or her life as their paramount consideration. Declining to recommend a match must remain a possible option.

What next?

A panel recommends whether a child should be placed for adoption with that particular prospective adopter and the agency then makes a decision about this. There is no provision for prospective adopters to make representations or to apply to the IRM if the match is not agreed.

Panel members should receive regular, perhaps three-monthly, reports on children placed but not yet adopted. Unfortunately, not all placements will work out successfully.

Disruption

Disruption statistics have not been routinely collected nationally. Adoption outcomes studies have considered children placed at different ages and for varying lengths of time, and so can be difficult to compare. Prior to the research study *Beyond the Adoption Order* (Selwyn *et al*, 2015), there was very little clarity about the number of adoption breakdowns, with the figure of up to 20 per cent in the case of older children often being quoted by Government, researchers and practitioners. The key findings of this research were that the national disruption rate for adoption over the 12-year timespan explored was 3.2 per cent, but that there was a variation in the rate between local authorities of between 0–7 per cent.

Argent and Coleman (2012) identified some common causes of disruption, including:

- key information is incomplete or unshared;
- inaccurate assessments of children's attachment patterns;
- impact of changes in the adoptive family;
- post-adoption depression in adopters;
- failure of therapeutic, health and education services to meet an expected need;
- poor interagency and interdepartmental communication;
- not enough support for foster carers to facilitate the move;
- an adult agenda rather than a child-centred introduction plan;
- not enough consideration of adopters' own children's needs and perspectives;
- lack of clarity and agreement about the purpose and management of contact;
- inadequate placement support;
- a lack of openness in the adoptive family;
- not enough preparation of the child for the move to permanence;
- not enough preparation of the prospective adopters to parent this particular child or sibling group.

Selwyn *et al* (2015), in their research, identified the following risk factors for possible disruption:

- where children were older at the point of entry to care;
- had had more moves whilst in care;
- were over four years of age when placed for adoption;
- where there had been a longer time period between the time of placement and the adoption order being made.

David Quinton (2012), in *Rethinking Matching in Adoptions from Care*, summarised from research that the characteristics of children that predicted potential disruption were:

- age at placement;
- grievance disruptions;
- maltreatment or rejection by birth parents;
- attachment to or disturbed contact with birth families.

Panel members should have the opportunity to consider and learn from placements that disrupt (see Chapter 2, *Agency policy and practice issues*).

In the event of a placement disrupting, good practice suggests that the family's approval should be suspended. If the family wishes to be considered for a further placement, the agency should conduct a review to consider their suitability to adopt in the light of the issues raised by the disrupted placement. This would be informed by findings and recommendations of the disruption meeting. There is no requirement to refer the case to panel unless the agency is considering a termination of approval. In this case, the agency should follow the procedures set out in regulations for considering new applicants, i.e. the family should see the new report before it is presented to panel and should have five days in which to comment. They will also have an opportunity, following the panel's recommendation, should the decision-maker be minded to terminate their approval, to make representations either to him or her or to the IRM. Panel members may also consider whether any further work is needed with the child to enable him or her to benefit from a further placement for adoption.

References

Argent H and Coleman J (2012) *Dealing with Disruption*, London: BAAF

Farmer E and Dance C with Beecham J, Bonin E and Ouwejan D (2011) *An Investigation of Family Finding and Matching in Adoption*, Adoption Research Initiative, London: DfE

Sellick C and Thoburn J (2004) *What Works in Adoption and Foster Care?*, London: Barnardo's

Quinton D (2012) *Rethinking Matching in Adoptions from Care*, London: BAAF

Selwyn J, Meakings S and Wijedasa D (2015) *Beyond the Adoption Order: Challenges, interventions and adoption disruption*, London: BAAF

6 Intercountry adoption

Introduction

Adoption in the UK is principally a service for children in the UK who need to be adopted and for those families coming forward to offer them a home. There are still many children being looked after by local authorities, who are waiting for adoptive families, and the focus of adoption work is to work with these children and to recruit, prepare and support new families for them. For many years a very small number of looked after children have been placed for adoption with relatives living overseas. Now, for the first time, legislation enables local authorities to identify some children whose needs may be met by adoption overseas even though no family is yet identified. The panel has a role in this and the process is described later in this chapter.

However, the majority of intercountry adoption cases being considered by panel are likely to be of prospective adopters in the UK wanting to adopt a child from overseas. All local authorities have a duty to ensure that a service is offered to these prospective adopters. However, some have arrangements with a local voluntary adoption agency that is registered to do this work, to do so on their behalf. There is usually a charge to the applicants for the work involved in the completion of a prospective adopter's report. This varies but many agencies charge around £6,000 or more. Many families want or only feel able to parent a young child without special needs and it is these families, among others, who often decide to try and adopt from overseas. The number of adoptions from overseas has remained fairly stable over the last few years at around 150 each year. This is a lower figure than previously, as countries overseas develop their own adoption services.

There has been a long-standing belief that all children should, wherever possible, be brought up within their family of origin or within a family of the same ethnic background, culture and nationality. Like in previous years, there are now far more international efforts to improve the lot of children and families in developing countries. However, this can often be accomplished only in the long term, and in the short term, intercountry adoption will meet the needs of some children. These adoptions should be arranged according to the highest possible professional standards, with everything possible done to protect the interests of the children involved.

Intercountry adoption can arouse strong feelings and does raise genuine moral and ethical dilemmas. There is a need for panel members to have time to discuss and address these. However, this is best achieved in a separate session, away from consideration of individual cases.

Agency policies and procedures

The agency will need to decide the following issues:

- whether to undertake intercountry adoption home studies itself or to arrange for a voluntary agency to do them for people in its area;

- whether to make a charge and, if so, how much and whether to have any exemptions to charging, e.g. for relatives;

- how existing agency policies that address the importance of assessing adoptive parents whose culture, ethnicity, religion and language match the child's as closely as possible will be taken into account;

- how policies on the importance for children of knowledge of their background and of some form of continuity with their past will be taken into account.

Considering and deciding whether a child should be placed for adoption outside the British Islands

(The British Islands are England, Wales, Scotland, Northern Ireland, the Channel Islands and the Isle of Man.)

For many years, arrangements have been made for some looked after children to be placed for adoption with families living overseas who are relatives of the child or known to them in some other way. This will still be possible, but under current legislation it is also possible, for the first time, for an agency (after a recommendation from the panel, provided that parents consent and there is no court involvement) to decide that a looked after child should be placed with a family living overseas even though no family has yet been identified. These latter placements must be made under the Hague Convention.

The "Hague Convention"

This is the shorthand description of the Convention on Protection of Children and Co-operation in respect of Intercountry Adoption. It was concluded in The Hague (Netherlands) in May 1993 and was finally ratified by the UK on 1 June 2003. Many other countries have ratified and implemented the Convention and new ones are doing so regularly. It is possible to check on whether the Convention is in force in a particular country on www.hcch.net.

Considering whether a child should be placed for adoption in a Hague Convention country

Panel involvement in considering the plan

The panel may be required to consider the adoption plan for the child under AAR 18 and The Adoptions with a Foreign Element Regulations (FER) 39 as it would for a child to be adopted in the UK. However, the restrictions on the panel considering a case apply equally to a looked after child who is to be adopted by prospective adopters from overseas (Guidance 2.64). (See Chapter 3 for all the information required and the issues to be considered.) However, *in addition*, the panel must ensure that:

- 'The child has been counselled about the adoption plan and that it has been explained to the child in an appropriate manner the procedures in relation to, and the implications of, an adoption in an overseas country' (FER 36 and AAR 13). The child must have had this information confirmed in writing.

- The child's birth parents must also have been counselled and must have had the implications of, and the procedures for, an intercountry adoption explained to them. This must have been confirmed in writing (FER 37 and AAR 14).

- The child's permanence report must include
    - a summary of the possibilities for placement within the UK (FER 38(a))
    - an assessment of whether an adoption by a person in a particular receiving state is in the child's best interests (FER 38(b) and AAR 17).

If no particular family has been identified at this stage, the panel will need to enquire very closely into what family-finding efforts have been made to explore the possibilities for placement within the UK. It is probable that positive recommendations are likely to be considered in cases where this will enable a child to be placed with adopters overseas who match the child's ethnicity and heritage. For instance, for a child born to people visiting the UK or living in the UK but retaining strong links to their country of origin, it might well be appropriate to consider adoption for the child with adopters in that country.

Possibly most of the positive recommendations made, however, will be in relation to children for whom a family in a Convention country has already been identified, i.e. relatives or someone known to the child.

Panel members should ensure that they check on how any contact arrangements will be organised. These may, of course, be facilitated by a placement in the country where most of the child's birth relatives live.

Issues of adoption support should also be considered. The Adoption Support Services Regulations 2005 will not apply overseas although financial support agreed could still be given by the child's agency.

When the panel is considering an intercountry adoption under the Convention it must consider and take into account:

- the Article 15 report (on the prospective adopters) if available, and the agency's observations on this (FER 39); and

- the assessment in the child's permanence report on whether an adoption by a person in a particular country is in the child's best interests.

What happens next?

If the panel has made a recommendation about whether or not a child should be placed for adoption in accordance with the Convention, a decision is made by the agency in the usual way. Notification is sent to the Department for Education (DfE) which is the Central Authority for England. The DfE will then arrange for brief anonymised details of the child to be placed on its Convention list of children in England available for intercountry adoption.

If the child's adoption agency subsequently decides that adoption overseas is no longer appropriate, it must notify the DfE, which will withdraw the child's name from the Convention list. Although there is no requirement for the panel to be involved in rescinding the plan, it would be good practice for the panel to be notified and agencies might choose to seek the panel's advice on changing the plan.

When an approved prospective adopter living in a Convention country outside the British Islands wishes to adopt a child from England, their country's Central Authority will forward their papers to the DfE. The DfE will check their details and will then consult the list of waiting children. It will look at the age and sex of the child and whether the child is part of a sibling group. The DfE will not be able to consider any additional details.

If there are any children available for adoption who appear, at face value, to link with the characteristics of the child the prospective adopters are approved to adopt, the DfE will send their papers to the child's agency.

The child's agency must consider the papers in the same way as any other match. If they need additional information, they must request this via the DfE. If they decide to pursue the match, it must be presented to panel, as described in the next section.

If the child's local authority decides not to pursue the match, it must return the papers to the DfE. The DfE will hold papers on families for six months before returning them to their agency overseas. They can be resubmitted at the request of the adopters.

The panel's involvement in considering a match with approved adopters from a Hague Convention country

The agency will have received a full report on the prospective adopters, prepared in their country. This is referred to as an *Article 15* report as it is prepared under Article 15 of the Hague Convention.

The adoption panel is required by FER 44 to consider the match under AAR 32 as it would for a domestic match. (See Chapter 5 for all the information required and the issues to be considered. The Article 15 report will take the place of the prospective adopter's report.) The agency must include their observations on the Article 15 report.

Panel members will need to give particular consideration to any arrangements for adoption support. The Adoption Support Services Regulations 2005 will not apply in the overseas country. However, any financial support agreed can continue to be paid by the child's agency.

Panel members will also need to be clear how any arrangements for contact will be organised.

As described in Chapter 5, many agencies invite prospective adopters to attend panel when the match of a particular child with them is being considered. It would be good practice to consider doing that in these cases too, where the prospective adopters know the child, although language issues and distance could make it difficult. It is not likely to be feasible in other cases because, at this stage, the prospective adopters will have very little detailed information on the child.

What happens next?

The agency makes a decision in the usual way. It must then prepare a report on the child, compliant with Article 16 of the Convention. This report goes to the DfE, which forwards it, via the foreign authorities, to the prospective adopters. If they decide to proceed, they travel to the UK to meet the local authority workers and the child. If both the local authority workers and the adopters want to proceed, the local authority must inform the DfE, which will liaise with its counterpart in the adopter's country. An agreement to proceed is reached and arrangements can then be made for the placement to proceed. The child will usually be adopted in the adopter's country. However, before the child can leave the UK, he or she must live in the UK with the adopters for 10 weeks. They must then apply to the High Court for parental responsibility or for a Convention adoption order. Until one of these orders has been granted, they cannot leave the UK with the child (Adoption and Children Act ss.84 and 85).

The panel's involvement in children's cases when the Hague Convention is not in force in the overseas country

The child and his or her birth parents are counselled in the same way as for a Convention adoption.

The child's permanence report should include a summary of possibilities for placing the child within the UK and an assessment of whether adoption by a person in a particular overseas country is in the

Effective Adoption Panels

child's best interests, as is required for a Convention adoption.

Good practice suggests that, provided the parents consent and there is no court involvement, the panel should consider whether the child should be placed for adoption in the overseas country, as described for Convention adoptions.

In a non-convention case, the agency should send details of the proposed placement and its reasons for proposing the placement to the panel. In these cases, the child's agency will have arranged for the prospective adopter to be assessed and prepared in their own country. The assessment should usually be carried out in the individual's state of origin and be sent to the agency for consideration in the same way as for any other prospective adopter. The child's agency may have done some of this work itself and, exceptionally, may have done all the work. Panel members should consider the approval of the prospective adopters in the usual way.

The panel should consider the match as described for Convention adoptions. This will be followed by an agency decision and arrangements to place the child. The prospective adopters will need to confirm that both of them (or only one if the agency agrees) will accompany the child on leaving the UK. Before the child can leave the country, the prospective adopters must live with the child for 10 weeks and they must then apply for parental responsibility to the High Court. They are not able to take the child out of the country unless this has been granted (Adoption and Children Act 2002, ss.84 and 85).

Considering prospective adopters

Panel members should refer to Chapters 1, 2 and 4 as they have the same responsibilities when considering prospective intercountry adopters as they do when considering those who wish to adopt a child in the UK. The process for panel consideration, the agency decision-making and the possible involvement of the IRM are the same, except that there are a few additional requirements in relation to prospective intercountry adopters.

The report on the prospective adopter must include:

(a) the state of origin from which the prospective adopter wishes to adopt a child;

(b) confirmation that the prospective adopter is eligible to adopt a child under the law of that state;

(c) any additional information obtained as a consequence of the requirement of that state; and

(d) the agency's assessment of the prospective adopter's suitability to adopt a child who is habitually resident in that state.

(FER 15(4) in relation to an adoption from a Convention country and very similar wording in AAR 30(3) in relation to a non-Convention country)

As for domestic adopters, the panel may give advice on the approval range for the prospective adopters. This will inform the agency's recommendation to the DfE once the agency has decided that the prospective adopters are suitable to adopt (AAR 30).

Although the same issues described in Chapter 4 should all be considered in relation to intercountry adopters, some are particularly significant for this group of prospective adopters and these are described below.

CoramBAAF has developed a form that can be used to assess intercountry adopters – PAR-ICA (England).

Issues relating to the family

Age

UK adoption law does not specify an upper age limit for adopters. However, age is relevant and an important factor for consideration. The applicant or both partners should have a reasonable expectation of retaining good health to meet the demands of a child during their adolescence and through to adulthood.

Many countries do have explicit guidelines on age limits, both upper and lower, and on the age gap between adopters and child. These are some of the individual differences in a country's procedure on which the panel will require information.

Marital status

In England and Wales, any couple in a committed relationship can apply jointly to adopt, whether or not they are married and whether or not they are of the same or different sex. However, some countries overseas may have different requirements and it will be important that this is clarified in the report.

Criminal record

Apart from certain specified offences that automatically bar people from adopting, criminal convictions are taken into account by UK agencies but will not necessarily mean that prospective adopters are not approved. Some other countries, e.g. China, rule out most people with a criminal record. This needs to be clarified in the report.

Issues of culture, "race", religion and language

Many, though by no means all, children adopted from overseas into the UK will be brought up by adoptive parents who do not share the child's heritage in terms of culture, "race", religion or language. All children will have been separated not only from their birth family but also from their country of birth.

Prospective intercountry adopters will need to demonstrate that they have knowledge and understanding of the culture, religion and history of the country from which they propose to adopt and, if possible and realistic, some knowledge of the language. They will need to know, or be prepared to get to know, adults from that country who share their child's heritage and who are willing to take on the responsibility of a significant role in the child's life to help him or her to develop a positive self-image and take pride in their heritage. The prospective adopters will need to have some understanding of racism and a willingness to recognise and to deal with their child's need to handle racism. Where will they go for help with this? Panel members will need to enquire carefully into these issues, keeping in mind that standards applied in cases of intercountry adoptions should be as rigorous as those in domestic adoptions.

Range of children for whom applicants wish to be considered

Children are linked with adopters from overseas in the child's country of origin. However, FER 4 and AAR 34 require the agency and the prospective adopters to share information on the child. The agency must meet and counsel the adopters about a possible placement of the child. They must be told about requesting an assessment for adoption support, and must be given the medical adviser's views on the likely health needs of the child.

When prospective adopters are applying in relation to a specific known child, probably a relative, as much information as possible about the child should be obtained by the agency. The assessment can then be focused on the prospective adopter's ability to meet that particular child's needs. In this situation the prospective adopter's report should name the child and give the date of birth. Approval will be in relation to that specific child. The Practice Note, *Adoption from Abroad of a Relative Child* (Howarth and Way, 2007), sets out the issues as well as pointers for good practice.

Health considerations in relation to children

Many children for whom intercountry adoption is considered have been abandoned or placed in institutions by parents who provide little background or medical information about themselves or the child.

Prospective adopters need to be aware that there may well be as yet unknown genetic factors which will have considerable implications for the child. Are the applicants prepared and able to cope with uncertainties about the child's future development? How will they cope should medical conditions become apparent after placement? Children may also have been exposed to the risk of conditions such as tuberculosis, HIV infection, Hepatitis B and C, among others. Reliable and safe testing may not be available in the child's own country. How capable will adopters be of parenting a child who may have a serious medical condition? Children may have experienced abuse and neglect and severe physical, intellectual and emotional deprivation. Are prospective adopters prepared for this and for the long-term and perhaps permanent harm that may have been done? It is particularly important for panel members to enquire about these issues as some prospective intercountry adopters choose to adopt a child from overseas rather than from the UK because they want a child who will be both young and also relatively "straightforward" and problem-free. CoramBAAF has produced a leaflet for intercountry adopters on these issues (see *Further Reading*).

The child's need for information

How aware are the applicants of the importance for children and young people of access to as much knowledge and information as possible about their birth family and the reasons for their placement? Do they understand the need to gather the information around the time of placement as this may be their only opportunity? Do they understand that the child's needs around this issue will change over time? How do they plan to meet these needs? Will they be able to help the child with his or her possible pain and anger that almost no information may be available? Do they view the lack of information and the unlikelihood of any possibility of contact with the child's birth family either now or in the future as a loss for the child and themselves or as a bonus? Sellick and Thoburn (2004) conclude that 'the successful adoptive parenting of children placed as infants is associated with the ability to accept the child's dual identity and the emotional significance which the family of origin will always have for the child and for themselves as substitute parents'.

Change of approval

Prospective adopters are approved as eligible and suitable to adopt a child from a specific country overseas. If the applicant wishes to apply to a different country after they are approved, there should be further discussion with the agency. An addendum report should be produced, which should evidence that the prospective adopter fully understands the cultural and other needs of a child from the "new" country. This report should be submitted to the adoption panel, which should make a fresh recommendation. This will go, in the usual way, to the agency decision-maker for a new approval.

Post-placement and post-adoption support

Children coming from overseas for adoption in the UK are potentially very vulnerable and may have a range of special emotional, developmental, health and educational needs. They and their families may well need, and are entitled to be assessed for, post-placement and post-adoption support. What will be offered by the agency and how receptive is the family to this? Are the applicants in touch with any support groups, such as Adoption UK or a specialist group for intercountry adopters? (See Appendix IV.)

References

Howarth G and Way J (2007) *Adoption from Abroad of a Relative Child*, Practice Note 52, London: BAAF

Sellick C and Thoburn J (2004) *What Works in Adoption and Fostering?*, London: Barnardo's

Further reading

BAAF (2004) *Children Adopted from Abroad: Key health and developmental issues*, London: BAAF

BAAF (2004) *Intercounty Adoption: Information and guidance*, London: BAAF

Selman P (ed) (2000) *Intercountry Adoption: Developments, trends and perspectives*, London: BAAF

Appendix I
Context of the agency's placement work

It will be helpful for central list and panel members to have some factual information about the area that the agency covers and about both the general population and the children looked after by the local authority. The following list of questions provides a useful format for a brief report to be included in the pocket on the inside back cover.

Local authorities

1) **Information on the agency and the panel**

- How many panels are there and what is their remit e.g. adoption only, adoption and permanence, fostering?
- Have the panel's roles and responsibilities changed recently?
- What volume of work does this panel deal with?
- Has this changed significantly in recent years?
- Are there any unusual aspects of the panel's work?

2) **Information on the area served (much of this should be available in statistics produced from census information)**

- What is the ethnic and cultural mix in the area?
- Are there areas that are unusual in terms of the ethnic and cultural mix within the area as a whole?
- What is the profile of the area in terms of:
  - the numbers of people with disabilities within the area?
  - employment/unemployment?
  - single parent families?
  - the housing mix?
  - youth justice issues?
  - poor school attendance?
  - general indices of poverty?
  - changes in population profile as a result of local government reorganisation?
- Do any localities stand out significantly in any of these respects?
- Have there been recent demographic changes?

3) **Information on the children**

- What is the percentage of children and young people in the population of the local authority as a whole?
- How many children are looked after?
- What percentage of children and young people in the general population of the local authority are looked after by the authority?
- How many of these are placed in local authority foster placements?
- How many are placed through independent fostering providers?
- How many are in residential care?
- How many are in agreed long-term foster placements?
- How many are placed for adoption but not yet adopted?
- How many are identified as needing adoption or a permanent placement but not yet placed?
- How many looked after children became the subject of a child arrangements order or a special guardianship order in the last year?

4) **Information on foster carers**

- How many foster carers does the agency have?
- How many of these are relatives of the child/young person placed?
- Is the pool of foster carers sufficient/insufficient to meet need?
- Are there particular groups of children/young people who are more difficult to place?
- Does the pool of short-term carers roughly equate in terms of ethnicity, culture, religion, language and class with the population of accommodated children and young people?
- Do the permanent carers approved through the panel roughly equate in terms of ethnicity, culture, religion, language and class with the population of looked after children and young people?
- Are the existing carers located close to the homes of the majority of the accommodated children and young people?

5) **Information on adopters**

- How many were approved last year
  - for domestic adoption?
  - for FFA or concurrency?

- for intercountry adoption?
- How many are approved and waiting for placements?
- How many have children in placement and not yet adopted?

Voluntary agencies

1) **Information on the agency and the panel**
- How many panels are there and what is their remit e.g. adoption only, adoption and permanence, fostering?
- Have the panel's roles and responsibilities changed recently?
- What volume of work does this panel deal with?
- Has this changed significantly in recent years?
- Are there any unusual aspects of the panel's work?

2) **Information about the area where the agency is located**
- Does the agency focus its activities mainly on this area?
- If not, what is the catchment area?
- Are there any geographical limitations?
- Do any geographical limitations relate solely to where referrals of children for family finding are accepted from or do they also relate to where referrals for potential families are accepted from?

3) **What is the focus of the agency's work?**
- Is there a particular specialism in terms of the kinds of children for whom the agency will family find?
- Is the agency contracted by a particular local authority to do specific work?

4) **Information on adopters**
- How many were approved last year
   - for domestic adoption?
   - for intercountry adoption?
- How many are approved and waiting for placements?
- How many have children in placement and not yet adopted?

Appendix II
Acts of Parliament, Statutory Instruments and Government Guidance

Acts   Abbreviations

The Adoption and Children Act 2002

The Children Act 1989   The Children Act

The Data Protection Act 1998

The Children and Families Act 2014

Statutory Instruments

The Adoption Agencies Regulations 2005 SI 2005 no. 389	AAR
The Adoption Agencies and Independent Review of Determinations (Amendment) Regulations 2011 SI 2011 no.589	
The Adoption Agencies (Panel and Consequential Amendments) Regulations 2012	
The Adoption Agencies (Miscellaneous Amendments) Regulations 2013	
The Restriction on the Preparation of Adoption Reports Regulations 2005 SI 2005 no.1711	ARR
The Suitability of Adopters Regulations 2005 SI 2005 no.1712	SAR
The Adoption Support Services Regulations 2005 SI 2005 no.691	ASR
The Adoptions with a Foreign Element Regulations 2005 SI 2005 no.392	FER
The Special Guardianship Regulations 2005 SI 2005 no.1109	
The Fostering Services (England) Regulations 2011 SI 2011 no.581	The Fostering Regulations
The Adoption and Children Act 2002 (Commencement no.10 Transitional Savings and Provisions) Order 2005 SI 2005 no.2897	The Transitionals Order
The Children Act Representations Procedure (England) Regulations 2006 SI 2006 no.1738	The Complaints Regulations
The Care Planning, Placement and Case Review (England) Regulations 2010 SI 2010 no.959	The Review Regulations
The Care Planning, Placement and Case Review and Fostering Services (Miscellaneous Amendments) Regulations 2013	
The Local Authority Adoption Services (England) Regulations 2003 SI 2003 no.370	
The Adoption and Children (Miscellaneous Amendments) Regulations 2005 SI 2005 no.3482	

The Adoption Agencies (Miscellaneous Amendments) Regulations 2014 (which amend the Adoption Agencies Regulations 2005 (the AARs), which make provision about the exercise by adoption agencies (that is, local authorities and registered adoption societies) of their functions in relation to adoption under the Adoption and Children Act 2002. They also amend the Care Planning, Placement and Case Review (England) Regulations 2010 (the CPPCRRs) and the Adoption Support Services (Amendment) Regulations 2014)

Government Guidance

Practice Guidance on Assessing the Support Needs of Adoptive Families (DfES, January 2005)

Special Guardianship Guidance under the Children Act 1989 (DfES, May 2005)

The Children Act Guidance, Volume 2, *Care Planning, Placement and Case Review* 2010

The Children Act Guidance, Volume 4, *Fostering Services*, 2011

Statutory Guidance on Court Orders and Pre-Proceedings for Local Authorities (DfE, April 2014)

Early Permanence Placements and Approval of Prospective Adopters as Foster Carers, Statutory Guidance for Local Authorities and Adoption Agencies (DfE, July 2014)

Statutory Adoption Guidance 2013 published by the DfE provides guidance for adoption agencies in England to the Adoption and Children Act 2002 and the Regulations and Court Rules. It was revised and issued as a draft document in 2014 to address changes included in the Children and Families Act 2014 but this version has not been finalised at the time of writing. It will only be quoted in this book where it covers issues not included in the 2013 version.

Standards

National Minimum Standards for Adoption [local authorities and registered voluntary adoption agencies] (2014)

National Minimum Standards for Fostering (2011)

Introduction to Adoption: National Minimum Standards 2014

The NMS, together with the adoption regulations, form the basis of the regulatory framework under the Care Standards Act 2000 for the conduct of adoption agencies and adoption support agencies.

The values statement below explains the important principles that underpin these Standards.

Values – children

- The child's welfare, safety and needs are at the centre of the adoption process.
- Adopted children should have an enjoyable childhood, and benefit from excellent parenting and education, enjoying a wide range of opportunities to develop their talents and skills leading to a successful adult life.
- Children are entitled to grow up as part of a loving family that can meet their developmental needs during childhood and beyond.
- Children's wishes and feelings are important and will be actively sought and fully taken into account at all stages of the adoption process.
- Delays should be avoided as they can have a severe impact on the health and development of the children waiting to be adopted.
- A sense of identity is important to a child's well-being. To help children develop this, their ethnic origin, cultural background, religion, language and sexuality need to be properly recognised and positively valued and promoted.
- The particular needs of disabled children and children with complex needs will be fully recognised and taken into account.
- Where a child cannot be cared for in a suitable manner in their own country, intercountry adoption may be considered as an alternative means of providing a permanent family.
- Children, birth parents/guardians and families and adoptive parents and families will be valued and respected.
- A genuine partnership between all those involved in adoption is essential for the NMS to deliver the best outcomes for children; this includes the Government, local government, other statutory agencies, Voluntary Adoption Agencies and Adoption Support Agencies.

Values – adopted adults and birth relatives

- Adoption is an evolving life-long process for all those involved – adopted adults, and birth and adoptive relatives. The fundamental issues raised by adoption may reverberate and resurface at different times and stages throughout an individual's life.
- Adopted people should have access to information and services to enable them to address adoption related matters throughout their life.
- Agencies have a duty to provide services that consider the welfare of all parties involved and should consider the implications of decisions and actions for everyone involved.
- Agencies should seek to work in partnership with all parties involved, taking account of their views and wishes in decision-making.
- Agencies should acknowledge differences in people's circumstances and establish policies that provide non-discriminatory services.
- Adopted adults have their adoptive identity safeguarded and the right to decide whether to be involved in contact or communication with birth family members.

(Reproduced from Department for Education (2014) *Adoption: National Minimum Standards*, London: Department for Education. This information is licensed under the terms of the Open Goverment licence. Available at www.education.gov.uk)

Appendix III
Glossary of terms

Accommodated/Accommodation

Under section 20 of the Children Act 1989, the local authority is required to "provide accommodation" for children "in need" in certain circumstances. The local authority does not acquire parental responsibility (see below) merely by accommodating a child and the arrangements for the child must normally be agreed with the parent(s), who, subject to certain restrictions, are entitled to remove the children from local authority accommodation at any time.

Adoption Link (part of Link Maker)

Adoption Link (part of Link Maker) offers a database of children waiting for adoption and approved adopters across the UK, and allows children's profiles to be searched by registered social workers and prospective adopters. There is a licence fee for local authorities. Adopters can also pay a one-off fee if their local authority does not subscribe to the scheme.

Adopters and family-finders create their profiles and load them onto the system. Family-finders can set specific criteria or limit families who can access the profile and can also look at families' profiles featured on the site.

Adoption placement plan

A plan that gives information to the prospective adopter about the child when the agency has decided to place the child with them. It sets out, for example, when the child will move into the prospective adopter's home, parental responsibility, adoption support services, contact with the child, and arrangements for reviewing the placement.

Adoption placement report

A report prepared by the adoption agency for the adoption panel that sets out, for example, the reasons for proposing the placement, arrangements for allowing any person contact with the child, the prospective adopter's view on the proposed placement, and, where the agency is a local authority, proposals for providing adoption support services for the adoptive family.

Adoption Match

Adoption Match is a national matching service, launched in July 2016 by Coram Children's Legal Centre. It organises activity days and exchange days and runs the Adoption Register for England (see below) on behalf of the Department for Education.

Adoption Register

An online database in England that stores the details of children waiting to be adopted and details of approved adopters who are waiting to be matched. A team of experienced social workers uses the database to link children with approved prospective adopters where local matches cannot be found.

Adoption Support Agency (ASA)

An organisation or person registered, under Part 2 of the Care Standards Act 2000, to provide adoption support services. An ASA may operate on a profit or not-for-profit basis.

Adoption Support Fund (ASF)

The Adoption Support Fund was established by the DfE in May 2015 following a pilot to provide funding for therapeutic services and therapies for children and families. Application to the fund is made by local authorities following an assessment of support needs being completed. The fund can be used for children living in England up to and including the age of 21 (or 25 with a statement of special educational needs or education, health and care plan) who are adopted and were previously in local authority care in England, Wales, Scotland and Northern Ireland, or who were adopted from overseas. In 2016 it was extended to also provide support to children on special guardianship orders.

Adult Attachment Interview (AAI)

A tool for assessing an adult's attachment style, based on asking about the adult's experience of being parented. It is used by trained assessors, largely as a research tool.

Article 15 report

Report prepared on the prospective adopter under Article 15 of the Convention on Protection of Children and Co-operation in respect of Intercountry Adoption (the Hague Convention). This includes information on their identity, eligibility and suitability to adopt, background, family and medical history, social environment, reasons for adoption, ability to undertake an intercountry adoption and the characteristics of the children for whom they would be qualified to care.

Article 16 information

Report prepared on the child under Article 16 of the Hague Convention. This includes information on his/her identity, adoptability, background, social environment, family history, medical history including that of the child's family, and any special needs of the child.

Attachment Style Interview (ASI)

A standardised assessment tool, developed at Royal Holloway, University of London, which can be used to assess the characteristics of carers in terms of their quality of close relationships, social support and security of attachment style. It assesses particularly the adequacy of support and the carer's ability to access support. It should only be used by trained assessors.

Brief report

If social workers come to the view, during a Stage Two assessment, that prospective adopters are not suitable to adopt, they may halt the process and prepare a brief report giving their reasons. This must be considered by the adoption panel and by the agency decision-maker. The agency decision-maker may require a full report to be prepared or may make a qualifying determination that the prospective adopters are not suitable. The prospective adopters can, if they wish, then apply to the IRM.

CAMHS (Child and Adolescent Mental Health Services)

Services that contribute to the mental health care of children and young people, whether provided by health, education or children's services or other agencies. CAMHS cover all types of provision and intervention from mental health promotion and primary prevention, to specialist community-based services.

Care order

See "In care".

Care plan

An agreed plan for looking after a child and meeting that child's current and future needs, made by the placing authority under the Children Act 1989. The care plan will be presented to court when a care order is applied for.

Care proceedings

The court process involved in consideration of whether or not to make a care order.

Central list

Adoption agencies must set up a central list of people who must be checked, inducted and trained, and from which the members of each panel must be chosen. Fostering service providers must do the same thing in relation to fostering panels.

Child Arrangements Order

An order under Section 8 of the Children Act 1989 settling the arrangements as to the person(s) with whom the child is to live. Where a child arrangements order is made in favour of someone who does not already have parental responsibility for the child (e.g. a relative or foster carer), that person will acquire parental responsibility subject to certain restrictions (e.g. they will not be able to consent to the child's adoption). Parental responsibility given in connection with a child arrangements order will only last as long as the child arrangements order. A child arrangements order can last until the child's 18th birthday.

Child Arrangements Order Allowance

Local authorities have a power (under Schedule 1 Para 15 of the 1989 Children Act) to contribute to the cost of a child's maintenance when the child is living with somebody under a child arrangements order provided that he or she is not living with a parent or step-parent. A financial contribution under this power is normally referred to as a child arrangements order allowance.

Children's guardian

A person working for CAFCASS who is appointed by the court to safeguard a child's interests in court proceedings.

Child's case record

A file that contains information about the child. This will include, for example, the child's permanence report, adoption panel's minutes, recommendation and advice given whether the child should be placed for adoption, agency decision, consent given or withdrawn, copy of placement order. The particular information to be kept is set out in AAR 12(1) and AIR 4.

Child's permanence report (CPR)

A report prepared by the adoption agency. This will include, for example, information about the child and his/her family, a summary of the state of the child's health, his/her health history and any need for health care; wishes and feelings of the child, his/her parent or guardian; the agency's view about the child's need for contact with his/her parents, guardian or any other person the agency considers relevant.

Child's review

Regulations prescribe that looked after children must have their care and the plans for them regularly reviewed. Reviews must happen, as a minimum, a month after the child starts being looked after, three months later, then every six months. Every major decision about a child should be considered at a review, including, clearly, the decision to start the adoption process.

Concurrent planning

This is the term given to a scheme in which children, usually babies or toddlers, for whom there is a chance that they might return home to their birth family, are placed with families who will foster them with this aim. However, the foster carers are also approved as adopters and will adopt the child should the planned return to the birth family not be successful. In this way, the moves that a child may otherwise have to make are minimised. These schemes have to be run with the agreement and co-operation of the local courts and to tight timescales.

Consortium

A group of usually not more than 6–8 local adoption agencies that share details of waiting families and children in order to try to make speedy local placements for children.

Contact/contact orders

Contact may be direct face-to-face contact between the child and another individual or it may be indirect, such as letters, often exchanged via the adoption agency by the child's adoptive parents and birth family members. This form of contact is often called letterbox contact. It is possible for a court to make a contact order requiring a specified form of contact, at the same time as or after the making of an adoption order. However, this is fairly rare.

Couple

Two people (whether of different sexes or the same sex) living as partners (married or unmarried) in an enduring family relationship. This does not include two people one of whom is the other's parent, grandparent, sister, brother, aunt or uncle.

Decision-maker

A senior person within the agency who is a social worker with at least three years' post-qualifying experience in child care social work. The decision-maker makes the final decision, after considering the recommendation of the adoption panel and, in some cases, of the independent review panel. There may be more than one decision-maker but all must be qualified as above.

Disclosure and Barring Service (DBS)

The organisation responsible for doing criminal records checks on behalf of employers and deciding whether it is appropriate for a person to be placed on or removed from a barred list. It can offer three levels of checks – a standard check of offences and cautions; an enhanced check that includes locally held police information; and an enhanced check that

Glossary of terms

includes checking the barred lists for children and adults. It replaces the CRB. Email: customerservices@dbs.gsi.gov.uk.

Fast-track approval process

This is available to anyone who is an approved foster carer in England and to people who have previously adopted in a court in England or Wales under the Adoption Agencies Regulations 2005 (or Welsh equivalent). It enables these individuals to enter the adoption approval process at Stage Two. Agencies are required to complete the process within four months.

Fostering/foster care

In this book, this term is used for those cases where a child is placed with a foster carer approved by the local authority (under Section 23(2)(a) Children Act 1989) or (in rare cases) placed directly by a voluntary organisation (under Section 59 (1)(a) of the Act). These placements are governed by the Fostering Services Regulations 2002. "Short-term", "long-term", and "permanent" foster care and "respite care" (also known as "short breaks") may mean different things to different people; they are not legally defined terms.

Fostering for Adoption (FFA)

The Care Planning, Placement and Case Review and Fostering Services (Miscellaneous Amendments) Regulations 2013 (which came into force on 1 July 2013) allow an agency to give an approved adopter temporary approval as a foster carer for a named child. This enables a child to be placed as a foster child with carers without them having had a full fostering assessment or panel approval as foster carers. These will be children for whom the likelihood of eventual adoption is high. However, the child is fostered until, in most cases, work with birth parents and court involvement enables an adoption plan to be agreed and the child to be matched for adoption with these carers at panel.

In care

A child who is subject to a care order under Section 31 of the Children Act 1989 is described as being "in care". A care order gives the local authority parental responsibility for the child but does not deprive the birth parent(s) of this. Nevertheless, the local authority may limit the extent to which parents may exercise their parental responsibility and may override parental wishes in the interests of the child's welfare.

Independent Review Mechanism – Adoption & Fostering (IRM)

A review process that is conducted by an independent review panel. The prospective adopter may initiate this process when their adoption or fostering agency has made a qualifying determination. The review panel reviews the case and gives a fresh recommendation to the agency.

Independent Reviewing Officer (IRO)

Chairs statutory child care reviews for looked after children. He or she is independent of the child's social work team and of budget holders.

Looked after

This term includes both children "in care" and accommodated children. Local authorities have certain duties towards all looked after children and their parents, which are set out in Part III and Schedule 2 of the Children Act 1989. These include the duty to safeguard and promote the child's welfare and the duty to consult with children and parents before taking decisions.

Open adoption

This term may be used very loosely and can mean anything from an adoption where a child continues to have frequent face-to-face contact with members of his or her birth family to an adoption where there is some degree of "openness" e.g. the birth family and adopters meeting each other once. People using the term should be asked to define what they mean!

Parental responsibility (PR)

All the rights, duties, powers, responsibilities and authority which by law a parent of a child has in relation to the child and his/her property. The most important elements of parental responsibility include:

- providing a home for the child;

- having contact with the child;
- protecting and maintaining the child;
- disciplining the child;
- determining and providing for the child's education;
- determining the religion of the child;
- consenting to the child's medical treatment;
- naming the child or agreeing to the child's change of name.

Placement order

An order made by the court under section 21 of the Adoption and Children Act 2002 authorising a local authority to place a child for adoption with any prospective adopters who may be chosen by the authority. It continues in force until it is revoked, or an adoption order is made in respect of the child, or the child marries, forms a civil partnership or attains the age of 18. Only local authorities may apply for placement orders.

Prospective adopter matching plan

A written plan to be completed once a prospective adopter has been approved as suitable to adopt. It should detail the process for matching a child, what the prospective adopter can do to identify a child, and the process for making representations to the agency.

Qualifying determination

In relation to *suitability to adopt a child* – a determination made by an adoption agency that it considers a prospective adopter is not suitable to be an adoptive parent and does not propose to approve him/her as suitable to be an adoptive parent.

Prospective adopter's report (PAR)

A report prepared by the adoption agency.

- *Full report* – includes, for example, the prospective adopter's date of birth, identifying information, ethnic origin, cultural/linguistic background, religious persuasion, description of his/her personality, whether he/she is single or a member of a couple, the agency's assessment of his/her suitability to adopt a child, and a summary of the prospective adopter's state of health.

- *Brief report* – the agency does not need to complete a full report where it receives information that leads it to consider that the prospective adopter may not be suitable to adopt a child. That information would be either that set out in Part 1, Schedule 4 of the AAR, or the health report, or the report of interviews with referees, or the local authority report, or other information.

Registration of Interest

This is a formal written request by an individual to enter Stage One of the adoption assessment process. The individual consents to the agency undertaking checks and confirms that they have not registered their interest with another agency. The agency should decide within five working days whether or not to accept the registration, unless there are exceptional circumstances which mean that longer is necessary.

Special guardianship

An order under the Adoption and Children Act 2002 offering an alternative legal status for children. The child is no longer looked after. It gives the special guardian parental responsibility, which he or she can exercise to the exclusion of others. However, the birth parent(s) retain parental responsibility. Support services, including financial support, are very similar to those for adopters.

Stage One – pre-assessment process

This stage of the adoption process starts once an agency has accepted a Registration of Interest from an individual. It should normally be completed within two months. Should it take longer, it must be recorded on the prospective adopter's case record. A Stage One plan should be agreed with the prospective adopter. Initial training and preparation will be given, and all prescribed checks and references will be carried out. Where an agency decides that a prospective adopter is not suitable to adopt during or at the end of this stage, it must inform the individual in writing with a clear explanation of the reasons. Prospective adopters may make a complaint, but have no recourse to the Independent Review Mechanism (IRM).

Stage Two – the assessment process

Prospective adopters are not able to start this part of the process until they have successfully completed Stage One. Stage Two should take four months to the final decision, unless there are exceptional circumstances or the prospective adopter asks for a delay. Reasons should be recorded on the case file. A written Assessment Plan should be prepared with the prospective adopter. This stage covers an assessment of the prospective adopter's suitability to adopt and should include any necessary intensive training. A prospective adopter's report (PAR) is completed, an adoption panel considers the case, and a decision-maker makes a final decision.

Twin-track, parallel or contingency planning

These are all names given to planning for a looked after child for adoption or long-term fostering while at the same time considering the possibility of placement with birth parents or with extended family members.

Appendix IV
Useful organisations

CoramBAAF

An organisation promoting best practice in both adoption and fostering services for children separated from their families. Its extensive publications are listed in a free catalogue or details are available at www.corambaaf.org.uk/bookshop. Consultants offer a phone and written advice and information service and also provide training for panels and for social work teams.
41 Brunswick Square
London WC1N 1AZ
Tel: 020 7520 0300
www.corambaaf.org.uk

Government departments

Department for Education
Ministerial and Public Communications Division
Department for Education
Piccadilly Gate
Store Street
Manchester M1 2WD
Tel: 0370 000 2288
www.education.gov.uk

Department of Health Publications (DH)
Ministerial Correspondence and Public Enquiries Unit
Department of Health
Richmond House
79 Whitehall
London SW1A 2NS
Tel: 0207 210 4850
www.gov.uk/government/organisations/department-of-health

Welsh Assembly Government
Children and Families Division
Cathays Park
Cardiff CF10 3NQ
Tel: 0300 060 3300
www.wales.gov.uk

Other organisations

Adoption Register for England
Works with agencies and consortia to make sure that children and families have the best chance of finding a suitable match.
Unit 4
Pavilion Business Park
Royds Hall Road
Wortley
Leeds LS12 6AJ
Tel: 0845 450 3931
www.adoptionregister.org.uk

Adoption UK
UK-wide self-help organisation for adoptive and prospective adoptive parents. Produces lots of helpful information, holds an Experience Resource Bank, and publishes a magazine, *Adoption Today*, with useful articles and details of children waiting for placement.
Units 11 and 12
Vantage Business Park
Bloxham Road
Banbury
OX16 9UX
Tel: 01295 752240
0844 848 7900 (helpline)
www.adoptionuk.org.uk

CAFCASS
The Children and Family Court Advisory and Support Service is a national non-departmental public body for England. CAFCASS is independent of the courts, children's services, education and health authorities and all similar agencies.
Tel: 0300 456 4000
www.cafcass.gov.uk

Children and Families Across Borders
A voluntary organisation that helps families and individuals whose lives are split between different countries.
Victoria Charity Centre
11 Belgrave Road
London SW1V 1RB
Tel: 020 7735 8941
www.cfab.org.uk

Useful organisations

Family Rights Group (FRG)
A national organisation that advises families which are in contact with children's services about the care of their children.
The Print House
18 Ashwin Street
London E8 3DL
Tel: 020 7923 2628
www.frg.org.uk

First4Adoption
This is a dedicated information service for people interested in adopting a child in England. (It cannot help with intercountry adoption or with fostering enquiries.) It has a helpful website that includes a list of agencies by area. Information helpline (0300 222 0022, 10am–6pm, Mon–Fri).

Fostering Network
Produces a wide range of leaflets, publications and training materials on all aspects of foster care and a quarterly magazine.
87 Blackfriars Road
London SE1 8HA
Tel: 020 7620 6400
www.fostering.net

Independent Review Mechanism (IRM)
A review process, conducted by a panel, that prospective adopters can use when they have been told that their adoption agency does not propose to approve them as adoptive parents.
Unit 4, Pavilion Business Park
Royds Hall Road
Wortley
Leeds LS12 6AJ
Tel: 0845 450 3956
www.independentreviewmechanism.org.uk

Intercountry Adoption Centre
Provides independent information and advice to anyone in the UK considering adopting a child from abroad, to adoptive families, adopted people and adoption professionals.
22 Union Street
Barnet
Herts EN5 4HZ
Tel: 0208 447 4753
www.icacentre.org.uk

Natural Parents Network (NPN)
National self-help organisation for birth parents who have parted with a child for adoption, run by birth parents. Provides information, support and counselling.
20 Rookery Way
Seaford
BN25 2TE
Tel: 0845 456 5031
www.n-p-n.co.uk

OASIS (Overseas Adoption Support and Information Service)
A UK-based voluntary support group for people who wish to adopt or who have already adopted children from overseas.
www.adoptionoverseas.org

Ofsted
The organisation responsible for registering adoption agencies and for inspecting adoption services every three years.

Post Adoption Centres

Organisations offering advice, counselling, information, training, and self-help and support groups to adopted people, birth families and adoptive families.

After Adoption
Unit 5 Citygate
5 Blantyre Street
Manchester M15 4JJ
Tel: 0161 839 4932
Helpline: 0800 056 8578
www.afteradoption.org.uk

After Adoption has a number of regional offices around the UK

PAC-UK

London:
5 Torriano Mews
Torriano Avenue
London NW5 2RZ
Tel: 020 7284 5879
www.pac-uk.org

Leeds:
Hollyshaw House
2 Hollyshaw Lane
Leeds LS15 7BD
Tel: 0113 230 2100
www.pac-uk.org

Appendix V
Sample job descriptions, evaluation and review formats

Sample job description and person specification for central list and panel members

Job description

1. To read the circulated papers carefully before the meeting and to attend the meeting prepared to raise issues and to contribute to the panel discussion.
2. To take responsibility for participating in the making of a recommendation, on each case, drawing on both personal and professional knowledge and experience.
3. To attend meetings of the panel as specified in your agreement with the agency.
4. To be prepared to attend additional panels if possible, if requested.
5. To participate, with other members, in advising on policy and procedural matters as required.
6. To address diversity issues and promote anti-discriminatory practice.
7. To safeguard the confidentiality of all panel papers and panel discussions.
8. To participate in induction and training, which will be at least one day per year.
9. To participate constructively in the annual review of your central list and panel membership.

Person specification

Experience and qualifications

- Experience, either professionally or personally or both, of the placement of children in adoptive and foster families or of children being cared for away from their birth family.
- A social work or medical qualification will be necessary for certain panel members. The two social work members must have at least three years' post-qualifying experience in child care social work, including direct experience in adoption work.

Knowledge

- An appreciation of the effects of separation and loss on children.
- Awareness of the richness of different kinds of families and their potential for meeting children's needs.
- Some understanding of the purpose and function of the panel and of the agency that the panel is serving or a willingness to learn.

Abilities

- Good listening and communication skills.
- The ability to read, process and analyse large amounts of complex and sometimes distressing information.
- The ability to make an assessment and to form a view, based on the written and verbal information presented to panel, and the confidence to articulate this at panel.
- The ability to use personal and/or professional knowledge and experience to contribute to discussions and decision-making in a balanced and informed manner.
- The ability to work co-operatively as part of a multi-disciplinary team.
- The ability to attend panel meetings as required, arriving on time, and to attend at least one training day each year.

Attitudes and values

- A commitment to keeping children within their own family or community where this is possible and to maintaining contact between children living in adoptive families and their birth families where this appears to be in the child's best interest.
- A commitment to adoption as a way of meeting a child's need for permanence, where this appears to be in the child's best interests.
- A valuing of diversity in relation to issues of ethnicity, religion, gender, disability and sexuality.
- An understanding of, and a commitment to, the need for confidentiality.
- A willingness to increase knowledge and understanding of issues through reading, discussion and training.
- A willingness to contribute constructively to the annual review of your central list and panel memberships and, as required, to that of other panel members and the Chair.

SAMPLE

Central list and adoption panel membership agreement

Name:

Agency:

Part 1 – The Central List Member

- I confirm that I have received and read a job description and person specification, and agree to comply with the points listed in the job description.

- I agree to participate in induction and training, which I understand will be at least one day per year.

- I agree to safeguard the confidentiality of records and information submitted to the panel and discussed at panel meetings.

- I agree:
    - to attend panel meetings as agreed with the agency;
    - to declare an interest and inform the Chair should I have knowledge, in either a personal or professional capacity, of a case under consideration;
    - to commit to anti-discriminatory practice and a preparedness to consider each case on its own merits;
    - to read the panel papers carefully and to come prepared to contribute to the panel discussion;
    - to arrive on time for panel meetings;
    - to consider attending an extra panel to deal with an urgent case;
    - to participate constructively in the annual review of my performance as a member and to discuss my continuing on the central list;
    - to inform the agency at once if I have been charged, cautioned or convicted for any criminal offence or if any criminal proceedings are pending;
    - to subscribe to the DBS online update service and to consent to the agency doing an online DBS status check as required (police check);
    - to give one month's notice in writing if I decide to resign from the central list;
    - to accept that the agency may give me one month's notice in writing, with reasons, that it is removing me from the central list.

Signed: **Date:**

Part 2 – The Agency

(It is likely to be either the agency adviser to the panel or the agency decision-maker who signs the agreement on behalf of the agency.)

Name of central list member:

Name and title of agency representative:

Agency:

- I confirm that a job description and person specification have been provided.
- I confirm that the agency will provide induction, training and written information, which will be updated as required, to keep the member 'abreast of relevant changes to legislation, regulations and guidance'. NMS 23.16
- At least an annual training day for all central list members will be arranged.
- Central list members will be given panel dates at least six months in advance, with confirmation as to which panels they are invited to attend.
- Individual support and help will be offered, as far as practicable, should the member need or request this.
- An annual review of the panel member's performance will be undertaken and discussion of their continuing on the central list.
- All the necessary information for each case will be sent at least five working days in advance of the date when the cases will be considered.
- Members will be assisted, if necessary, in the provision of a suitable, secure storage space for confidential panel papers while they are in the panel member's home.
- Travel costs will be reimbursed and the payment of a fee for reading panel papers and panel attendance will be discussed with the member. The amount to be paid will be confirmed in writing.
- An opportunity will be made available for members to make representations or complaints to the agency.
- Any concerns about a panel member's behaviour or conduct in the panel will be discussed informally and, if necessary, at an additional review. If these concerns cannot be resolved, the agency will put in writing the reasons why it is ending the panel member's appointment. One month's notice in writing will be given.

Signed: **Date:**

Review of central list and panel members

Introduction

A review of the performance of all central list and panel members is required by statutory Guidance 1.35 and 1.36. This must happen at least annually and must be conducted by the agency adviser to the panel and the panel Chair. (See Chapter 1 for more information.)

An additional review could be convened, as required, by the agency or the member.

Preparation for the review

- The member should complete a self-evaluation form (see following page).

- The panel adviser and/or Chair should prepare a summary of any comments made by presenting social workers, service users or other panel members.

- Both the member and the agency adviser and Chair should check and reflect on the issues in the member's panel agreement (see section in Chapter 1) and on any job description and person specification that the member has had.

At the review

The member, the Chair and the panel adviser should meet and should go through and discuss

- the self-evaluation form

- the summary of comments made

- the panel agreement, and job description and person specification, if applicable.

A written summary should be made and signed by the panel member, the Chair and the panel adviser.

After the review

The written summary and the supporting documents should be kept on the member's personnel file.

SAMPLE

Self-evaluation form: central list and panel member

What do you think are your strengths as a panel member?

Is there anything you would like to change or improve in your performance as a panel member?

Do you have any suggestions about how this could be done?

Are there any factors which prevent you being as effective as you would like to be as a panel member?

Do you have any suggestions about how these could be addressed?

Self-evaluation form: central list and panel member

Self-evaluation form: central list and panel member

Is there any specific input or training that you would find helpful?

Do you have any comments about the general functioning of the panel or about the management of the central list?

Do you have any suggestions for how it could be improved?

Please comment on the strengths and any limitations of the Chair of the panel.

Please comment on the strengths and any limitations of any other panel members.

Signed: Date:

SAMPLE

Review form: central list and panel members

Date: Name:

Date of inclusion on the central list:

Dates or frequency of panels attended in the last year:

Strengths as a panel member

Areas for change and/or development by the panel member

How and by when will these be achieved?

Any changes to be made by the agency

How and by when will these be achieved?

Input and training planned

Signed central list/panel member: Date:
Agency adviser to the panel: Date:
Panel Chair: Date:

Review form: central list and panel members

SAMPLE

Job description and person specification for panel Chair

Job description

1. To chair panel meetings, ensuring that all items of business are covered and that the panel operates in accordance with Regulations and Guidance and the policies and procedures of the agency.

2. To prepare for panel meetings, reading panel papers carefully, identifying key issues and alerting the agency adviser if necessary to ensure, as far as possible, that the case is adequate for submission to panel.

3. To facilitate the active participation of all panel members in contributing to the panel's consideration of cases and to the making of clear and well-evidenced recommendations with the reasons for these.

4. To ensure that all those attending panel are treated with respect and courtesy.

5. To address diversity issues and to promote anti-discriminatory practice at all times.

6. To ensure that clear and accurate minutes are written, which record any serious reservations that panel members may have, and to be involved in checking and agreeing minutes with other panel members before they are sent to the decision-maker.

7. To liaise with the decision-maker and with other senior managers as required.

8. To ensure, with the agency adviser, that senior managers are aware of issues of concern, in relation both to individual cases and to more general matters.

9. To be involved as appropriate in the recruitment and appointment of central list and panel members and in any consideration about terminating the appointment of a member.

10. To review, with the agency adviser, the performance of central list and panel members as the need arises, and at least annually.

11. To assist in developing, promoting and monitoring policies and procedures and high standards of work in adoption and permanence services in the agency.

12. To assist in planning training for members and to participate in this at least one day per year.

13. To safeguard the confidentiality of all panel papers and panel discussions.

14. To be involved in:

- deciding whether a case is adequate for submission to panel;
- deciding on the attendance of observers at panel;
- deciding on the participation of a panel member who declares an interest in a case;
- deciding when an extra panel may be necessary;
- preparing an annual report on the panel's work.

Person specification

Experience and qualifications

- Experience, either professionally or personally or both, of the placement of children in adoptive and foster families and of children being cared for away from their birth family.
- Experience of chairing complex meetings.

Knowledge

- An appreciation of the effect of separation and loss on children.
- Awareness of the richness of different kinds of families and their potential for meeting children's needs.
- An understanding of the purpose and function of the panel and of the agency that the panel is serving.

- An understanding of the adoption process and of the legislative framework for the work of the panel, or the capacity to develop this knowledge quickly.

Abilities

- The authority and competence to chair a panel, ensuring that the business is covered and that the panel operates in accordance with Regulations, Guidance and the policies and procedures of the agency.

- Excellent interpersonal and listening skills.

- The ability to communicate well and clearly both verbally and in writing.

- The ability to process and analyse large amounts of complex and sometimes distressing information.

- The ability to identify key issues and possible solutions and to communicate these clearly.

- The ability to facilitate the active participation of all panel members in contributing to the panel's consideration of cases and recommendations.

- The ability to ensure that those attending panel are communicated with respectfully while also ensuring that panel members are able to explore any concerns they may have openly and honestly.

- The ability to manage the expression of strongly held but possibly conflicting views by panel members and to help the panel to reach a recommendation which takes account of all these views.

- The ability to take up issues as required with the agency, liaising with the decision-maker and other senior managers.

- The ability, working with the agency adviser, to review each central list and panel member's performance when required, and at least annually, ensuring that this is a helpful and constructive process for both the member and the panel as a whole.

Attitudes and values

- A commitment to keeping children within their own family or community where this is possible and to maintaining contact between children living in adoptive families and their birth families where this appears to be in the child's best interest.

- A commitment to adoption as a way of meeting a child's need for permanence, where this appears to be in the child's best interests.

- A valuing of diversity in relation to issues of ethnicity, religion, gender, disability and sexuality.

- An understanding of, and a commitment to, the need for confidentiality.

- A willingness to increase knowledge and understanding of issues through reading, discussion and training.

- A willingness to contribute constructively to the annual review of their role as panel Chair.

SAMPLE

Adoption panel Chair agreement

Name:

Agency:

Part 1 – The Chair

- I confirm that I have received and read a job description and person specification and agree to comply with the points in the job description.
- I agree to participate in induction and training which I understand will be at least one day per year.
- I agree to safeguard the confidentiality of records and information submitted to the panel and discussed at panel meetings.
- I agree to participate constructively in the review, with the agency adviser, of all members on the central list, to take place at least annually and more often as required.
- I agree to participate as required in regular meetings with the panel adviser and decision-maker to discuss and raise general issues in relation to panel and agency work and practice.
- I agree to be involved, with the panel adviser, as necessary in deciding whether reports are adequate for submission to panel.
- I agree to be involved, as required, in the preparation of an annual report on the panel's work.
- I agree to do my best to chair meetings to time, to involve all panel members, to facilitate the participation of social workers and prospective adopters, and to ensure that clear and well-evidenced recommendations are reached.
- I agree to participate in a review, at least annually, of my performance as Chair, to be undertaken by the decision-maker.
- I agree to give one month's notice in writing if I decide to resign as panel Chair and central list member.
- I accept that the agency may terminate my appointment as Chair and as a central list member by giving me at least one month's written notice, with reasons.
- I agree to subscribe to the DBS online update service and to consent to the agency doing an online status check as required.

Signed: **Date:**

Part 2 – The Agency

(It is likely to be either the agency decision-maker or the agency adviser to the panel who signs this agreement on behalf of the agency.)

Name of Chair:

Name and title of agency representative:

Agency:

- I confirm that a job description and person specification for the Chair have been provided.
- I confirm that the agency will provide induction, training and written information, which will be updated as required to keep the Chair 'abreast of relevant changes to legislation, regulations and guidance'. NMS 23.16
- At least an annual training day for all central list members will be arranged.
- Panel dates will be agreed with the panel Chair and arranged for a year ahead.
- Individual help and support will be offered, as far as practicable, should the Chair need or request this.
- Regular meetings with the panel adviser and decision-maker will be scheduled for general discussion of issues in relation to panel and agency work and practice.
- An annual review of the Chair's performance will be undertaken by the agency decision-maker, which will include discussion of their continuing as Chair.
- Expenses and payment for the work undertaken will be discussed and agreed and confirmed in writing.
- Any concerns about the Chair's behaviour or conduct in the panel will be discussed informally and, if necessary, at an additional review. If these concerns cannot be resolved, the agency will put in writing the reasons why it is ending the Chair's appointment. One month's notice in writing will be given.

Signed: **Date:**

Review of panel Chair

Introduction

A review of the performance of the panel Chair is required by statutory Guidance 1.35 and 1.36. This must happen at least annually and must be conducted by the decision-maker. (See Chapter 1 for more information.)

An additional review could be convened, as required, by the decision-maker or the panel Chair.

Preparation for the review

- The panel Chair should complete a self-evaluation form (see following page)
- The panel adviser should prepare a summary of any comments made by presenting social workers, service users or other panel members.
- Both the panel Chair and the agency decision-maker should check and reflect on the issues in the Chair's panel agreement (see section in Chapter 1) and on any job description and person specification which the Chair has had.

At the review

The Chair and the decision-maker should meet and should go through and discuss

- the self-evaluation form
- the summary of comments made
- the panel agreement, and job description and person specification if applicable.

A written summary should be made and signed by the Chair and the decision-maker.

After the review

The written summary and the supporting documents should be kept on the Chair's personnel file.

SAMPLE

Self-evaluation form: panel Chair

What do you think are your strengths as a Chair?

- In panel meetings
- In your performance of the other responsibilities of the Chair

Is there anything you would like to change or improve in your performance as a Chair?

- In panel meetings
- In your performance of the other responsibilities of the Chair

Do you have any suggestions about how this could be done?

Are there any factors which prevent you being as effective as you would like to be as a panel Chair?

Self-evaluation form: panel Chair

Do you have any suggestions about how these could be addressed?

Is there any specific input or training that you would find helpful?

Do you have any comments about the general functioning of the panel?

Do you have any suggestions for how it could be improved?

Signed: **Date:**

SAMPLE

Review form: panel Chair

Date: Name:

Date of inclusion on the central list:

Dates or frequency of panels attended in the last year:

Strengths as a panel Chair

Areas for change and/or development by the panel Chair

How and by when will these be achieved?

Any changes to be made by the agency

How and by when will these be achieved?

Input and training planned

Signed panel Chair: Date:

Agency decision-maker: Date:

SAMPLE

Checklist of additional information that may be provided by the agency

Please tick if included

- ☐ List of central list members (with brief details and email addresses/phone numbers)
- ☐ Name, job title and email address/telephone number of the professional adviser
- ☐ Name and job title of the agency decision-maker
- ☐ Central list and panel agreement for members
- ☐ Format for undertaking the annual review of central list and panel members
- ☐ Context of the agency's placement work (see Appendix I)
- ☐ The latest annual report of the panel, if one is produced
- ☐ The latest management report detailing activity levels in the agency's adoption work
- ☐ The latest set of policy and procedures for adoption work, prepared under Regulation 7 of the Adoption Agencies Regulations 2005
- ☐ Any other relevant policies not included in the above
- ☐ Arrangements for considering long-term fostering situations
- ☐ Information on the assessment and preparation process for applicants, including the programme for groups
- ☐ Relevant extracts from Children's Services Plan
- ☐ Child care or permanence policy
- ☐ Equal opportunities policy
- ☐ Child Protection policy

Any other information

- ☐
- ☐
- ☐

Book list

Adoption stories

Real-life stories written by adopters who have experienced the highs and lows of adoption at first hand.

Our Adoption Journey, **by Jayne Lilley** (2016)
A true story of a couple's path to adoptive parenthood, following Jayne, Dan and their son Charlie as they adopt a young baby girl.

An Adoption Diary, **by Maria James** (2006)
A true story of an adoption, following Maria's and Rob's journey to adopting a two-year-old child, and the highs and lows along the way.

Flying Solo, **by Julia Wise** (2007)
Inspiring and accessible, this book describes the realities of life on your own with an adopted child, with practical hints and tips.

In Black and White, **by Nathalie Seymour** (2007)
This honest account follows a white couple living in 1970s Britain who adopted two black children, describing how the children settle in, get to know their birth relatives and eventually decide to leave their adoptive home.

Adoption Undone, **by Karen Carr** (2007)
The true story of an adoption and an adoption breakdown, bravely told by the adoptive mother as she looks back at what went wrong and why.

Together in Time, **by Ruth and Ed Royce** (2008)
From a dual perspective, the authors look back on their decision to adopt a boy with attachment difficulties, the fear that their family was falling apart, their experience of music and art therapy, and their decision to adopt for a second time.

The Family Business, **by Robert Marsden** (2008)
A revealing story of the adoption of William, a little boy with cerebral palsy, by a middle-aged couple with three birth children, and the effects on their family life.

Take Two, **by Laurel Ashton** (2008)
This candid account reveals the author's personal heartache at her infertility, the emotional and physical demands of IVF; how and why the decision to adopt two young girls is the right choice for this family in waiting.

I wish I had been Born from You, **by Karen Lomas** (2009)
Written by a mother, with contributions from her adopted daughter, this heartfelt collection charts a moving and emotional adoption journey of getting to know one another and becoming a family.

Frozen, **by Mike Butcher** (2010)
Written by an adoptive father, this honest and humorous account explores the lengths to which one couple go to create their dream of a family. It provides a shocking exposure of how IVF treatment can go horribly wrong and reveals how a flyer from an adoption agency changes the couple's life.

When Daisy met Tommy, **by Jules Belle** (2010)
The story of how six-year-old Daisy and her parents adopted Tom. Although written by her mother, Daisy's thoughts and feelings about the family's decision to adopt, and her perspective on the process, are vividly brought to life.

Is it True you have Two Mums?, **by Ruby Clay** (2011)
The heart-warming story of Ruby and Gail and their belief in their potential to adopt. Some social workers they encounter think that, as a lesbian couple, they are unfit to be parents; others recognise that their Asian dual-heritage family has much to offer. This account charts their journey to becoming parents to three adopted daughters.

Becoming Dads, **by Pablo Fernández** (2011)
Set against a contemporary backdrop of diverse perceptions – both encouraging as well as hostile – as to whether gay men should adopt, Pablo's narrative tracks their journey, from their own initial doubts about whether or not they would be accepted, through to the positive affirmations they receive and their adoption of a young boy.

As if I was a Real Boy, **by Gordon and Jeannie Mackenzie** (2011)
The inspirational story of how Gordon, who was 10 and living in a psychiatric hospital with undiagnosed mental health issues, was adopted by Jeannie. In a moving account, mother and son look back at how adoption changed their lives for the better.

Anthologies

Adopters come together to share their experiences.

***Loving and Living with Traumatised Children*, by Megan Hirst** (2005)
Based on the experiences of nine individuals who adopted traumatised children, this book looks at the "co-operative enquiry" they set up to investigate the effects of trauma on themselves.

***Looking After our Own*, edited by Hope Massiah** (2005)
This inspiring collection looks at the experiences of nine adoptive families and their children, exploring their motivation to adopt, what their social workers had to offer or not, the roles of friends and family, and what adoption has meant to them.

***Proud Parents*, by Nicola Hill** (2013)
A compelling and poignant collection of stories of lesbians and gay men who have adopted or fostered children. They share their experiences on what motivated them, the assessment process, what it was like when the children moved in and what life as a family is like.

Adoption guides

***Advice Note:* Intercountry Adoption** (2006)
This short guide describes the intercountry adoption process and includes: information on the reasons it is sometimes used; some of the issues and implications for families involved; and basic practical guidance on procedures and rules.

***Panel Members Considering Applications from Prospective Lesbian or Gay Adopters or Foster Carers*, by New Family Social** (2013)
This booklet provides information for panel members on lesbian and gay adoption and fostering, the outcomes for children, and various points to consider when considering applications.

***Adoption Conversations*, by Renée Wolfs** (2008)
This in-depth practical guide explores the questions adopted children are likely to ask, with suggestions for helpful explanations and age-appropriate answers. Although the guide focuses primarily on the needs of children adopted from abroad, the practical advice is applicable to any adopted child.

***More Adoption Conversations*, by Renée Wolfs** (2010)
This in-depth practical guide explores the problems that adopted teenagers (up to 18 years old) are likely to confront and provides suggestions for helpful solutions and achievable communication methods.

***The Pink Guide to Adoption for Lesbians and Gay Men*, by Nicola Hill** (2012)
This essential step-by-step guide, the first of its kind to be published in the UK, explores the adoption process and examines how being a prospective lesbian or gay adopter can and does affect every aspect of this. Illustrated throughout with quotations and true stories.

***Related by Adoption*, by Hedi Argent** (2012)
This popular handbook gives grandparents-to-be and other relatives information about adoption today, how it will affect them, and the positive roles they can play.

***Talking about Adoption*, by Marjorie Morrison** (2012)
This popular and comprehensive guide outlines the whys, whens and hows of telling the truth about an adopted child's origins, based on the experiences of many people who have been adopted, and adopted parents.

By adopted children and adults

What do children think about adoption? How do adopted adults feel their lives have been affected?

***Chosen*, edited by Perlita Harris** (2012)
This anthology brings together essays and poetry by over 50 adopted adults, capturing a wide range of perspectives on identity and belonging, loss and grief, roots and searching, and family and relationships.

***The Colours in Me*, edited by Perlita Harris** (2008)
A unique collection of poetry, prose and artwork by adopted children and young people. Over 80 contributors – ranging from four to 20 years of age – tell it like it is, revealing what it feels like and what it means to be adopted.

***Readings from The Colours in Me* DVD** (2008)
Filmed on location at The Drill Hall in London, this inspirational and thought-provoking DVD features readings by 30 children and young people who

contributed to BAAF's popular anthology The Colours in Me.

Special and Odd, by James Mulholland (2007)
In this revealing and extraordinarily witty memoir James Mulholland tells the story of how he met his birth mother 29 years after being given up for adoption.

Mother Me, by Zara H Phillips (2008)
In this intensely personal and compelling memoir, Zara H Phillips examines her relationships with her adoptive and birth mothers, and invites the reader to join her in her own journey to become a mother.

The Birth Father's Tale, by Andrew Ward (2012)
Thirty years after his son was adopted, Andrew Ward set out on a journey to resolve the past. He describes his search for his son and illustrates how being a "birth father" has affected his relationships, career decisions and attitudes.

Just a Member of the Family DVD (2005)
This is the first film about adoption from a child's point of view, and features a number of birth children talking about how they were prepared and prepared themselves for an adopted child joining the family.

Panel information

Thinking of Joining an Adoption Panel?, by Sarah Borthwick and Marion Hundleby (2016)
This leaflet provides advice and information for anyone who may be going to join an adoption panel.

Attending the Adoption Panel as a Presenting Social Worker, by Jenifer Lord (2016)
This leaflet describes how presenting social workers can prepare for attending panel.

Prospective Adopters Attending Adoption Panel, by Jenifer Lord (2016)
This leaflet provides guidance for panel members on the prospective adopter's role in a panel meeting, the level of impact they can have and how their contribution should be evaluated.

Thinking of Joining a Fostering Panel?, by Pat Beesley (2016)
This leaflet contains an introduction to the role and remit of a fostering panel.

A Guide to Writing Panel Minutes, by John Pratt (2016)
This leaflet will help panel minute-takers to meet statutory requirements and produce accurate and high quality minutes.

These pamphlets can be purchased, or are available free to individual and agency members in the members' area of the CoramBAAF website, at www.corambaaf.org.uk.

Handbooks

The Attachment Handbook for Foster Care and Adoption, by Gillian Schofield and Mary Beek (2006)
This comprehensive and authoritative book provides an accessible account of core attachment concepts, enabling readers to understand the kind of caregiving in foster and adoptive families that can help children to feel more trusting, confident, competent and secure.

A Child's Journey through Placement, by Vera Fahlberg (1994)
Separation, loss, grief and change are experiences common to children requiring permanent placements. This essential reference book contains the theoretical knowledge base and skills necessary for understanding, working with, and planning for these children and their families.

The Child Placement Handbook, edited by Gillian Schofield and John Simmonds (2009)
This authoritative collection captures a wealth of knowledge and wisdom across diverse child placement issues, from the impact of abuse and neglect prior to placement to the challenges of providing support.

From the Ten Top Tips series

A series that looks at some fundamental issues and good practice points.

Making Matches, by Jennifer Cousins (2011)
Considers the needs of both children and adults, how these impact on the matching process and how a balance in meeting both can be maintained, with an emphasis on developing practice.

Placing Children, **by Hedi Argent** (2006)
Explores the issue of child placements, with an emphasis on evidence from practice and clear accounts of what works and what does not.

Placing Siblings, **by Hedi Argent** (2008)
Explores the different, often conflicting, principles involved in placing looked after siblings, including when to keep siblings together or help them to part; listening to each child and getting to know the group; and using kinship care.

Supporting Adopters, **by Jeanne Kaniuk with Eileen Fursland** (2010)
Describes the legal framework for adoption support and the principles on which a successful support service depends, along with information on financial support, supporting the wider family, managing children's difficult behaviour and contact.

Good Practice Guides

Adoption by Foster Carers, **by Elaine Dibben and Viv Howorth** (2016)
This practice guide makes a powerful case for considering the benefits of foster carers adopting children in their care, exploring how to prepare and assess carers, the matching process and effective adoption support.

Placing Large Sibling Groups for Adoption, **by Hilary Saunders and Julie Selwyn** (2013)
This guide is based on a study which examined the experiences of adopters parenting a sibling group, and presents recommendations for best practice in handling the adoption process.

Dogs and Pets in Fostering and Adoption, **by Paul Adams** (2015)
Explores the benefits and challenges of dogs and other pets for fostered and adopted children, and issues to be considered during the assessment process.

Planning for Contact in Permanent Placements, **by Paul Adams** (2012)
Explores the purpose of contact and what should be considered when assessing and formulating contact plans for children moving into permanent placements, including kinship placements.

The Role of Special Guardianship, **by John Simmonds** (2011)
Focuses on the key issues that need to be taken into account in relation to special guardianship assessments, planning, process and support, with information about the use of special guardianship to fulfil children's needs for a permanent placement.

Evaluating Obesity in Substitute Carers, **by Mary Mather and Karen Lehner** (2010)
Provides considered information and advice about how to assess obesity and associated health issues, alongside many other factors, in order to reach a balanced view about the potential benefits and drawbacks of placements for children and assessments of adopters and carers.

Exploring Infertility Issues in Adoption, **by Ian Millar and Christina Paulson-Ellis** (2009)
Infertility is frequently a motivating factor behind an adoption application, and its impact on a successful assessment and a good match between adopter and child should be considered. This guide examines how to consider infertility as part of the assessment process.

Concurrent Planning, **by Sarah Borthwick and Sharon Donnelly** (2013)
Explores what concurrent planning entails, how this can be a positive choice of placement for certain children, the legal and practice background, how it fits into care planning pathways, and how to assess concurrent carers.

Social Work with Gypsy, Roma and Traveller Children, **by Daniel Allen and Paul Adams** (2013)
Provides a comprehensive introduction to social work in this field, and includes information about Gypsy, Roma and Traveller communities, the social policy context, anti-discriminatory casework, and placement issues, including the assessment and support of adopters and carers.

Together or Apart?, **by Jenifer Lord and Sarah Borthwick** (2008)
Highlights factors which affect decisions on whether siblings are placed together or separately, and considers when, how and by whom key decisions are made.